$3.75

D1083410

James M Davies
Col 3:16

Sing . . . with Understanding

JAMES P. DAVIES

Sing . . .
with Understanding

Published by

COVENANT PRESS

Chicago, Illinois

to

my wife Louise, who sings "with the
spirit and with the understanding also"
and whose spirit of understanding, together with sacrificial encouragement,
made this work possible . . . with love.

Foreword

One of the more encouraging aspects of today's revolution in church life is a revival of interest in liturgical practice. This goes far beyond a renewed appreciation of the church calendar or of the symbolism in church architecture and decoration. Basically, it seeks to reverse the trend toward spectatorism in which we simply "listen" to sermons and prayers and to involve everyone in active worship. This is a practical demonstration of the Reformation doctrine that every believer is a "priest unto God."

Nevertheless, we seem to be losing ground in the one area of involvement in which evangelicals have traditionally excelled. For the most part, our congregations *do not sing well!* Many reasons have been given—the trend to shorter services, the new emphasis on graded choirs, and so on. Many churches have seemingly forgotten that hymns and hymn singing should be taught just as carefully as the Lord's Prayer or the Apostles' Creed.

There are notable exceptions, of course, and the historic First Covenant Church of Minneapolis, Minnesota, is one. As minister of music, James P. Davies has demonstrated his conviction that the heart of church music is what the congregation sings for itself. He has made *The Hymnal* of the Evangelical Covenant Church come alive for that congregation. And now, through this volume, he is sharing that ministry with Christians in many denominational fellowships.

His own preface emphasizes that this is not a "hymnal companion" in the traditional sense. Statistical background information on each of *The Hymnal's* selections can be found in other volumes. This book offers much, much more and has to be recognized as unique in many ways.

In choosing a number of hymns to be studied in depth, Mr. Davies draws attention to the subject divisions of *The Hymnal* and also presents an overview of historic hymnody. The Greek and Latin authors are here, along with their greatest translator, John Mason Neale. The German Reformation hymnists Luther and Rinkart are presented, as well as Isaac Watts, Charles

Wesley, Reginald Heber, Henry van Dyke, Charlotte Elliott, Philip Bliss, Fanny Crosby, and many more.

Most hymnologists fail to adequately acknowledge our debt to the Scandinavian writers. In this book, the reader and singer can become well acquainted with such spiritual and literary giants as A. L. Skoog, Lina Sandell, Carl Boberg, and Hans Adolph Brorson.

The musician shares honors here with the poet. Hymn-tune writers—Johann Crüger, Joseph Barnby, John B. Dykes, Lowell Mason, Wm. H. Doane, Ludvig M. Lindemann, and Oscar Ahnfelt, for example—are recalled and their contributions evaluated.

It should not be thought that this is merely a collection of biographies or hymn stories. Mr. Davies recognizes that circumstances and inspiration may have contributed greatly to the birth of a hymn. But he is more concerned with what it may say to today's worshipper than what it may have meant to yesterday's author. For him, the church's songs are doctrinally relevant, not theologically pedantic. Hymn tunes, the organization of a hymnal, and all our techniques of hymn singing are only tools which should make the text come alive in human experience.

In it all, the author escapes the artist's temptation to take himself, or even his message and mission, too seriously. Good humor is mixed with sagacious advice. Church music—like the gospel of Jesus Christ—is for all the people. This volume exhibits a love of people that transcends a love of the art or even of the institutional church. We believe it is this attitude that will best be used to help our congregations "sing with the spirit, and . . . with the understanding also."

DONALD P. HUSTAD

Louisville, Kentucky
September, 1966

Contents

Foreword by Donald P. Hustad vii

Preface xi

1. An Introduction to *The Hymnal* 1

2. Adoration 15

3. Times of Worship 21

4. The Holy Trinity 28

5. God the Father 31

6. Jesus Christ the Lord 39

7. The Holy Spirit 57

8. The Holy Scriptures 61

9. Invitation and Salvation 64

10. The Life in Christ 73

11. The Church and the Sacraments 92

12. The Kingdom of God on Earth 98

13. Heaven and Homeland 109

14. Children's Hymns 114

15. Special Seasons and Services 117

Index 125

Preface

When the song leader says "Let's sing," he is usually very happy if most of the people will do just that. Too often there is a considerable sprinkling of worshipers who are content to sit out the hymn sessions with closed mouths, thereby not only failing to contribute but by their silence discouraging their neighbors from participation as well.

We have placed a premium upon the "everybody sing" aspect of congregational song, and well we should. The Psalmist said, "Let *all* the people praise" (Psalm 67:3). The current predilection for volume also has scriptural encouragement: *"Make a loud noise,* and rejoice, and sing praise" (Psalm 98:4). Even the organist whose volume of sound antagonizes can find some justification in Psalm 33:3: "Play skilfully *with a loud noise."* Certainly hearty participation is a desirable goal.

But is this sufficient? The Apostle Paul said, "I will sing with the spirit, and I will sing *with the understanding also."* The Revised Standard Version reads, "I will sing *with the mind* also." Perhaps we should add to our singing invitation, "Let's *think!"*

John Wesley had quite a lot to say about full and hearty singing. "Sing *lustily,"* he said, "and with a good courage. Beware of singing as if you are half-dead or half-asleep; but lift up your voice with strength." He also instructed: "Sing *all.* See that you join with the congregation as frequently as you can. Let not a slight degree of weakness or weariness hinder you. If it is a cross to you, take it up, and you will find it a blessing."

But Wesley was also concerned about the mental aspect of singing. He instructed his early Methodist preachers to interrupt a noisy hymn and ask questions of the congregation: "Now do you know what you said last? Did it suit your case? Did you sing it as to God, with the spirit and understanding also?"

This recalls for me a unique experience of some years ago while serving under the ministry of the late Pastor Gustaf F. Johnson. The congregation was singing with customary lassitude a familiar song containing some strong statements of personal commitment. I was leading the singing with habitual aplomb when suddenly I felt a heavy hand on my arm and heard a stentorian voice calling out "Stop! stop!" The music came to an abrupt halt. He continued, "Stop lying! Think of what you are singing. We will sing the song again, and only those who mean what they are singing will sing." After recovering from the shock, we repeated the song, somewhat subdued but undoubtedly more thoughtful.

Our songs have many purposes. We may sing in adoration of the attributes of God, in thanksgiving for His goodness to us, in penitence for our shortcomings, in praise of His Word, in admonition to the lost, in testimony of His great salvation and our experience of His grace. But we do not do all this at one time. The motivation of each song should determine our heart attitude, and this should control our interpretation of the hymn. Not all singing should be loud. Sometimes it might even be silent! Perhaps the one who does not "join heartily in the singing of the last stanza" is "singing and making melody in his heart to the Lord." I say *perhaps!*

It is to encourage more to "sing . . . with understanding" that this book is written. It is not a hymnology textbook, nor is it a complete hymnal commentary, although it is hoped it may whet the appetite for such weightier tomes. It is a study of a hymnal, specifically *The Hymnal* of the Evangelical Covenant Church of America, but in a practical sense it goes far beyond denominational confines. It is a cross-section view of Christian hymnody, with the familiar and the unfamilar, the old and the new, the light and the profound, gospel song and standard hymn all standing side by side.

These are not "hymn stories" as such, although there are many accounts of how the hymns were written and used. They are not biographies, even though there is much vital information about the writers of our hymns. They consist of what stands out to the gaze of one worshiper as he opens his hymnal. This worshiper owes everything to the research of scores of people, plus a lifelong enriching exposure to the hymnody of a number of different Christian groups.

He would like to mention the recent assistance of one man through whose help was unlocked many treasures of the Scandinavian hymn heritage. Dr. Obed Johnson, retired missionary and college professor, spent many hours in putting on tape his lucid English translations and condensations of passages from Oscar Lövgren's three-volume Swedish work, *Våra Psalm- och Sångdiktare*. Through his delightful and brilliant assistance considerable information concerning the Swedish hymnists is appearing in English for the first time.

It is sincerely hoped that each reader will be counted among that glorious company who—from the time "when the morning stars sang together" till that day when "they sing the song of Moses the servant of God, and the song of the Lamb"—"sing with the spirit and . . . with the understanding also."

JAMES P. DAVIES

Minneapolis, Minnesota
September, 1966

"Sing therefore, ye Christians. Rekindle that sacred glow in your souls at the holy altar of song. Sing peace into your own hearts. Sing the doubting and hesitating ones into the presence of Christ. While we are still on this earth our song should continually grow stronger, more joyful and more rich in meaning. If thus we sing here and now, our song before the throne of God when we have entered into 'life more abundant' will be doubly glorious. The Lord entrusts sacred song to human lips. It is a God-given privilege to sing with gladness of heart, as a beautiful testimony to our Christian faith and devotion."

OSCAR LÖVGREN

Sing . . . with Understanding

Chapter One

An Introduction
to *The Hymnal*

Thanksgiving Day in colonial America is frequently represented pictorially by a painting of an early pilgrim on his way to church. A musket is over his shoulder, and a book is under his arm. One might at first assume that the book is the Bible, but a study of the times would reveal that it is more likely the Psalter—the *Bay Psalm Book*. This historic volume—the first book to be printed in the New World—was the worshiper's most important aid, and the family fortunate enough to own one cherished it highly.

We no longer bring a hymnal to church today; it is provided for us in the pew. But it is still the most important tool in our worship experiences.

Many of us who were brought up in the nurture of the church have cut our teeth on it—literally! It is frequently a fan. We have all fingered it, shared it, sometimes mutilated it. It is the most identifying feature of the sanctuary. A visitor may find it to be the only object of familiarity. It is the common denominator of worship. Next to the Bible itself, it is the Christian's most familiar book: the hymnal.

When Martin Luther, under God, defied the existing ecclesiastical hierarchy and restored the belief in the universal priesthood of believers, he made available two great tools to insure the practice of this relationship: the Bible and the hymnal. He gave his countrymen the Bible in their own tongue that God might speak *directly* to them. He gave them the hymnal that they might answer *directly*. He said, "Next to theology I give the first and highest honor to music."

Spiritual leaders of the more than 400 years since Luther's day have borne the same witness to the supremacy of hymnody—next to the Word of God itself. And indeed it is, in large part, the Word of God set to music.

Henry Ward Beecher put it this way: "Hymns are the jewels which the Church has worn, the pearls, the diamonds, the precious stones, formed into amulets more potent against sorrow and sadness than the most famous charm of the wizard or the magician. And he who knows the way that hymns have flowed, knows where the blood of true piety ran, and can trace its veins and arteries to the very heart."

The roots of the hymnal lie deep in Jewish soil. That first compilation of sacred song, the Psalms, records God's earliest dealings with man. In the Christian era the body of hymnody has not only accompanied the progress of the church, but it has helped mold that progress. In the fourth century the Arian heresy was fought by the hymns of Ephraim in the East and Ambrose in the West. Luther's use of music in his reformation has already been referred to. Its effectiveness is attested by his enemies, who lamented that "his hymns have damned more souls than his sermons!" In the Wesleyan awakening, the hymns of Charles were fully as potent as the sermons of his brother John. Indeed, at the forefront of most of the great movements have been a pair of leaders with the twin ministries of the Word and music. Moody had his Sankey, Torrey his Alexander, Billy Sunday his Homer Rodeheaver. The "Swedish Moody," E. A. Skogsbergh, had also his musical counterpart in A. L. Skoog. All used and made their contribution to the hymnal.

Through the pages of the hymnal march the literary and musical leaders of the world. On the left, or text, side of the page one sees names such as Bunyan, Tennyson, Lowell, Longfellow, Bryant, Holmes, Whittier, and Wordsworth. On the musical right frequently appear the masters, such as Bach, Beethoven, Handel, Haydn, Mendelssohn, Schumann, Sibelius, Mozart, and Weber. The rich spiritual experiences of hundreds of people are reflected in its lines. And not the experiences of poets and preachers alone, but of kings, industrialists, scientists, farmers, housewives, and sailors. The songs that fill the sanctuary on a Sunday morning were written in a wide variety of situations: on horseback, in classrooms, in dungeons and jails, in hospitals, parlors, trains, and ships.

True ecumenicity is nowhere better revealed than in the hymnal. Here opposing poles of theological opinion find a common expression of shared truth that transcends dogma. The contemporary hymnologist, Ernest Edwin Ryden, exults in the panorama of "true believers of all centuries, climes and communions, though divided by language, customs, doctrines, traditions and many other barriers, worshiping and adoring the same God and Lord with a united voice."

This is the book we take in hand each Sunday morning. It is a book stained with the blood of martyrs and the tears of saints, hallowed by the echoing voices of millions who have shared its canticles, saturated with the memories of many personal spiritual experiences, and sanctified by the Spirit of God himself, whose Word illumines every page.

Yet this book, rich treasury that it is, familiar to the point of being commonplace, is almost never studied, seldom seen outside the confines of the pew. A few pages are used somewhat perfunctorily once or twice a week; much of it is never used. The average worshiper knows very little about it. It is the book everybody uses and nobody knows.

It is the desire to remedy this condition that prompts the writing of this volume. Not that one could assemble in such small confines more than fragments of the treasures which cluster about the hymnal. But there is the sincere hope that the presentation of a few assorted gems may instill a continuing interest that may make jewel collectors of us all.

WHAT DO WE FIND IN THE HYMNAL?

A standard hymnal is much more than a collection of hymns. We want to rule out immediately many commercial publications which have made claim to the status of hymnal but have borne but a superficial resemblance to the real thing. They customarily lack the dignity, the scope and balance of material, as well as the organization and helps found in a true hymnal. They usually contain too many contemporary gospel songs (of which the publisher generally owns the copyright) to the exclusion of many of the tested hymns of past centuries. They often evince little planning, a hymn of penitence frequently appearing adjacent to a hymn of praise. Their indexes are usually too few and inadequate. I recall finding in the topical index of one such book the song "The Church in the Wildwood"—the very inclusion of which would be questionable—listed under invitation hymns!

Today there seems to be an encouraging shortage of these tawdry song collections which were formerly foisted upon would-be worshipers. A number of the very houses which produced these in large quantities during the early part of the century are now putting forth some quite creditable hymnals worthy of the name. For churches whose denominations do not provide worthy or adequate hymnals, these books serve very well.

Another encouraging sign is the production of some very fine hymnals by some of the smaller denominations, many of whose churches have traditionally used the cheap commercial publications. This is to be fostered since only in this way can church groups raise hymn standards and also preserve certain heritages peculiar to each denomination.

We are using as our model *The Hymnal* of the Evangelical Covenant Church of America, 1950, published by Covenant Press of Chicago. It has the format typical of the standard denominational hymnal and is quite comprehensive in its sampling of the great body of Christian hymnody while consciously preserving the hymn heritage of its own tradition.

HYMNS LISTED BY SUBJECT

After the customary Foreword, Preface, and Acknowledgements, the body of the volume is given over to the hymns themselves, grouped under sixteen broad categories (a seventeenth consists of several nonmusical Aids to Worship), with some fifty-four subheads. These subjects, which are also in the upper right corner of each page, are helpful guides in the selection of hymns, supplemented by the Topical Index. The entire scheme of subject groupings is listed in the Table of Contents in the front of the book.

THE INDEXES

There are eleven indexes available for our use in *The Hymnal*, considerably more than the average hymnal.

The *Index of Translations from the Swedish* deals with one of the unique features of *The Hymnal* of the Evangelical Covenant Church: the large body of Swedish hymns. There are 81 of them, and they are listed here alphabetically, together with the Swedish title.

The *Index of Swedish Texts* lists those seven Swedish hymns of which the entire Swedish text has been included.

The *Index of Authors, Translators and Sources* lists the names, together with the birth and death dates, of those connected with the texts of all the hymns in the book. In cases of anonymity, national origins or the name of the volume in which the hymn was first found are usually given. Much valuable information is available here for the interested reader. Here we can note that 1970 is the 150th anniversary of Fanny Crosby's birth. Her married name is also given: Mrs. Alexander Van Alstyne, together with the thirteen hymns which are included in *The Hymnal.*

A glance through this index reveals many interesting facts. One can note, for example, that John Quincy Adams, sixth president of the United States, wrote a hymn. It's the rarely used "Send Forth, O God, Thy Light and Truth." The maze of dates reveals that some texts have come down to us from the early centuries of the Christian era. The earliest: "Shepherd of Tender Youth" (No. 192), written by Clement of Alexandria, whose dates are c. 170 - c. 220. The list of hymn credits shows the largest number following the name of E. Gustav Johnson, who has translated some 23 hymns from the Swedish. Among the actual authors, Charles Wesley leads with 16 hymns.

The *Index of Composers, Arrangers and Sources* identifies those responsible for the music. A roving look along its columns reveals a number of facts: the oldest tune, listed merely as "Ancient Plainsong," dates back to the thirteenth century. The most prolific, so far as representation in *The Hymnal* is concerned, is Lowell Mason, American music education pioneer. The second largest list identifies the tunes by the best of the Victorian tune composers, John Bacchus Dykes, closely followed by the ubiquitous "Anonymous"! It is also interesting to note that the traditional folk tunes of seventeen nationalities are included.

The *Alphabetical Index of Tunes* might be nominated by some as the best list of useless information. Others find it quite fascinating and useful. These are the identifying names given by the composers (or hymnal editors) to their tunes. Seldom stereotyped and often capricious, they can stimulate interesting research. Sometimes they are derived from a phrase of the text most frequently associated with the tune, as *The First Nowell*, or *Beautiful River*. The phrase may be in the original language, as *Loven Herren*, *Ar Hyd Y Nos*, or *Ein' Feste Burg*. It may be the name of the author of the associated text, such as *St. Theodulph*, or *Dix*. Often it is the name of the composer: *Mendelssohn*, or *Darwall*. At times it may be the name of a person somehow associated with the writing of the tune, as in the case of *Beecher*, the pastor of the church where the composer was organist; or *Rathbun*, a soprano in the composer's choir, honored because she was the only one to show up one particular Sunday morning! It may be a town or even a street where the composer made his residence, illustrated by *Chautauqua* and *Federal Street*. And, occasionally, it may have a rather exotic origin, such as *Ton-Y-Botel*, literally "tune in a bottle," from a Welsh legend that this melody was found on a piece of paper stuffed into a bottle washed up on the Welsh coast during a storm.

The *Metrical Index of Tunes* is, to the uninitiated, a list of meaningless hieroglyphics. It is a grouping of the various hymn tunes by their metrical, or syllabic, structure. The standard meters: Short Meter (6. 6. 8. 6.), Common Meter (8. 6. 8. 6.), and Long Meter (8. 8. 8. 8.) are listed by their initials (S. M., C. M., and L. M.) together with more irregular metrical patterns. The number of digits indicates the number of lines per stanza, and each digit is the number of syllables in each line. The addition of the letter D indicates that the pattern should be doubled. For example: 8. 7. 8. 7. D. would mean 8. 7. 8. 7. 8. 7. 8. 7.

The chief value of this information is probably the facilitation of exchanging texts and tunes. This is not as common a practice in America as in some other countries, but it can serve practical purposes.

Let us illustrate what is meant by exchanging texts and tunes. Any Long Meter tune can be sung to any Long Meter text. It may not always sound particularly good, but it can be done. For example, the familiar Doxology, "Praise God from Whom All Blessings Flow," is in Long Meter. In other words, it has four lines of eight syllables each. Any other Long Meter text can be sung to that tune, known as *Old Hundredth*. We will scan the list of Long Meter tunes in the Metrical Index and look up the hymns indicated. Let's try a few. *Hamburg* is usually associated with the text "When I Survey the Wondrous Cross." Try singing these words to the *Old Hundredth* tune. Although they don't sound too appropriate, they do fit. The same is true of "Jesus Shall Reign" (usual tune: *Duke Street*). The converse, however, is better. This would mean that we should sing "Praise God from Whom All Blessings Flow" to *Duke Street*, the usual tune for "Jesus Shall Reign." There is a fine lilt and lift to the tune that adds variety and interest to the familiar text. The possible combinations are almost infinite, and very interesting.

The purposes of such transpositions are generally for interest and convenience. Sometimes one finds a certain text very appropriate for a particular occasion, but the tune is not familiar enough to assure good congregational participation. The substitution of a familiar tune may save the day. Some ministers have found this so practical that they do it quite frequently. There are dangers here, however:

1. Too frequent changes can be confusing, even to a trained congregation. Some will be irritated by the practice.
2. Constant substitution of familiar tunes for unfamiliar

tends to stunt the congregation's normal musical growth.

We must remember that the text and tune combinations selected for *The Hymnal* were considered by a competent committee of editors as the most appropriate, and their choices should be honored. This should not deter us, however, from occasional experimentation.

In the choral area this practice becomes more important and useful. Choirs are more adaptable to change, and there is frequently more need for variety. Let us demonstrate by giving two illustrations.

A special missionary banquet theme was chosen and turned over to the minister of music to find appropriate music. The theme "Links of Light" conveyed the idea of Christians around the world united by their common faith in Christ in spite of many human differences. The picture was that of a golden chain uniting all believers. Was there a song illustrative of this thought? "Golden chain . . . golden chain . . . golden *cord* . . . 'golden cord close binding all mankind.' " The song was soon identified as Oxenham's "In Christ There Is No East or West" (No. 501). A most appropriate hymn! But the tune, *St. Peter*, although an excellent one for congregational use, didn't offer much in the way of choral possibilities.

The Metrical Index to the rescue! After considerable experimenting with different Common Meter tunes, we finally decided on *Vox Dilecti*, normally used with the text "I Heard the Voice of Jesus Say" (No. 239). Since it is a Common Meter doubled tune, it was possible to sing two stanzas of "In Christ There Is No East or West" to one rendition of the tune, making it possible to use all four stanzas without monotony since the tune need only be sung twice.

A simpler illustration is in the divorcing of "What a Friend We Have in Jesus" (No. 364) from its over-familiar and not too stimulating tune and uniting it with the rich cadences of *Ton-Y-Botel* (No. 449, 500), often called *Ebenezer*. The result is electrifying. Our relationship with the divine Friend is transformed from a somewhat maudlin sentimental yearning to a rugged, vibrant experience!

The *Index of Responses* is a listing of the service music included as a special section in *The Hymnal*. A suggestion might be in order here that the director should not confine himself to this section in his search for responses. There are many hymns which make fine responses. An entire stanza, or perhaps merely a phrase, becomes very effective for this purpose.

The list of *Hymns Suitable for Choir Use* is a fine guide for the choral director to hymns which lend themselves particularly well to choral use. Some of the most effective anthems are those sung directly from *The Hymnal*, with occasional variety through the use of descants, free organ accompaniments, and changes of voicing.

The *Index of First Lines of Stanzas of Hymns* is a listing which many do not realize is available in *The Hymnal*. Here we have an alphabetical list of the first lines of all stanzas of all hymns. Perhaps you recall a hymn which contains the phrase "A glory gilds the sacred page," but you can't find it. The reason is that this is the second stanza of the hymn listed as "The Spirit Breathes Upon the Word." This index enables you to find it quickly.

The *Topical Index* is possibly the most useful of all indexes for the minister or the musician seeking to find just the *right* hymn for an occasion. Here we have 175 separate headings, with many cross-references, covering most subjects and occasions requiring appropriate hymns. This is about as complete as such a listing can be, but one must remember that many hymns cover more than one subject and that what may have an appropriate title may branch off into another area. Perhaps one or two stanzas of a particular hymn may fit your need perfectly, omitting the others. No index can replace careful and prayerful study, but this index in particular can greatly assist such a study.

The *Index of First Lines, Refrains and Familiar Titles* is certainly the most used of all the indexes. The traditional practice in hymnody is to use the first line as the title, but there are many exceptions to this, particularly in the modern gospel song era. The editors of *The Hymnal* have tried to restore the standard procedure. So, for example, you will find the song you may think of as "Faith Is the Victory" listed as "Encamped Along the Hills of Light." The italicized titles in the index take care of that problem since these are the familiar titles, usually the first phrases of the refrains.

STUDY OF A SINGLE PAGE FORMAT

We look now at the information given on a page of *The Hymnal*. At the extreme upper right corner we have the general classification of the hymn, following the outline given in the table of contents.

Below that, and at the left margin of the page, is given the *hymn number*. In the interests of proper nomenclature, note that this is not the *page number*. In some hymnals there is a separate page number given at the bottom of the page, in the center. Because some pages may contain two hymns and some hymns may occupy more than one page, these numbers rarely coincide.

Centered along the same line is the *hymn title*, that is, the name of the text. This consists of all or part of the first line of the hymn. Some hymnals are not at all consistent in this matter, mixing first lines with other types of titles. For example, "O Beautiful for Spacious Skies" is sometimes titled "America the Beautiful."

Directly below the hymn title is given the *tune name*. We

have discussed this practice under the *Alphabetical Index of Tunes*. Many gospel songs have been given no specific name for their tunes. Our hymnal editors have supplied these, usually selecting some identifying phrase from the text.

Below the tune name we find the *metrical analysis*, given either by the popular abbreviations (C.M., L.M.D., etc.) or by the numerals indicating the actual number of syllables per line (6. 5. 6. 5.).

The next line gives the information regarding the *origins of the text and tune*. On the left we see the author's name, followed by the year in which the hymn was written—if known. If the text is of foreign origin, the name of the translator is also given. The name of anyone making substantial alterations or additions appears here also. In the event that the names are not known, some other information is given. For example, "K" in Rippon's "Selection," 1787, identifies "How Firm a Foundation" (No. 328) by the collection in which it first appeared. Failing to find any information, the editors will resort to "Anonymous." This occurs only rarely in *The Hymnal* since a great deal of research has gone into the matter of origins.

Across the page, on the same line as the textual origins, is given the name of the composer, the arranger, and/or any other appropriate information, including date of composition.

A feature of *The Hymnal* not often found in such volumes comes next, given at the left side of the page just before the printing of the musical score. This consists of an *interpretive suggestion* regarding the singing of the hymn. This word or phrase helps to establish the proper mood for effective hymn singing. Given in English, these are simple and direct, such as: "Quietly with flowing rhythm," "With energy," or "Jubilantly." It is hoped that all hymn singers, as well as organists, take note of the suggestions.

Next comes the hymn itself, with the text printed between the musical staves. Some few hymnals still follow the practice of putting the music at the top of the page and the text given as a poem below. Most American hymnals have abandoned the practice as not conducive to the best congregational singing. It might be well to note that the music of the hymns is generally a four-part vocal score. Only in rare cases is there an instrumental accompaniment part given. "Ancient of Days, Who Sittest Throned in Glory" (No. 59) is one of these exceptions. A very interesting exception is the hymnal of the Covenant Church of Sweden, *Sånger och Psalmer*, 1951, in which all the hymns —all 788 of them!—are written in instrumental accompaniment form. In most hymnals, however, the organist or pianist is expected to adapt the vocal score to the proper instrumental style. In most cases this would consist of little more than a regrouping of the chord tones and the possible addition of octave doublings in the bass. When the music demands, *and the accompanist's ability allows*, this may develop into a full-scale free accompaniment. These accompaniments should be developed along traditional, tasteful lines. It should be needless to say that popular music stylings have no place in the worship service. There are several excellent collections of free organ accompaniments available which set desirable patterns for the more elaborate treatment of hymn playing. Another warning: whenever it is desired to use changes in chords, the congregation should be advised to sing in unison.

At the end of the hymn score may or may not appear an "amen." This may or may not be used! The practice of congregations differs in this regard, and rarely do we find a consistent, intelligent approach. It would seem that there are in general but two prevalent practices: (1) To sing the "amen" *always*, or (2) to sing the "amen" *never*. A variation in the former practice might be that it is to be sung following the first hymn on Sunday morning only. There could be interesting points of debate in this area, but they cannot be treated here. Sufficient to say that when sung in the spirit of the hymn, the addition of the "amen" can be a fitting close to a canticle addressed to God. "Tacked on" to a didactic hymn or gospel song, it can be most inappropriate.

At the very bottom of the page appears information regarding the copyrights and permissions. This would not seem to be of any interest to the average user of *The Hymnal*, and in most cases it is not. The person who may on occasion want to copy, whether by hand or mechanical process, words or music from *The Hymnal*, should be advised of the copyright facts.

The important facts can be stated quite simply. If nothing appears at the bottom of the page, the hymn is in the public domain and can be used freely by anyone. If the hymn is copyrighted, that copyright affects both text and musical score. Neither can be copied, together or separately, by any process whatsoever, without permission of the owner. Nor can such a song be arranged or adapted without permission. A copyright is valid for twenty-eight years, at which time it may be renewed for another twenty-eight years. After this time it is in the public domain and cannot be copyrighted in that form again. An arrangement of a public domain song may be copyrighted, however. It is sad to note that many church duplicating machines, not to mention pens and blackboards, are frequently put to illegal use.

Copyright laws are currently undergoing reviewal, and there may be important changes appearing soon. Needless to say, churches should be alerted to the law's provisions and regulations—and should abide by them.

Chapter Two

Adoration

*I saw ... the Lord sitting upon a throne, high and lift-
ed up, and his train filled the temple. . . . Holy, holy,
holy is the Lord of hosts: the whole earth is full of his
glory.*
—Isaiah 6:1, 3

It is not for alphabetical reasons that "Adoration" is the
first section of *The Hymnal*. The prime purpose of sacred
song is worship, and the keynote of worship is adoration.
The word is a glorious admixture of praise, love, and reverence. It is often debased, as are many transcendent words,
in conversational speech. A woman may say she "simply
adores" her new dress. This is almost sacrilege. Such a word
should be reserved for Deity. In it is enough awe to raise it
above the human and enough sincere devotion to keep it
securely linked to the heart.

The most satisfying division of Christian song, as far as I
am concerned, is this:

1. Songs in which man speaks to God about God.
2. Songs in which man speaks to God about man.
3. Songs in which man speaks to man about God.

There is a fourth category in which man speaks to man
about man. These songs in praise of human experience have
no place in true Christian hymnody. We had better avoid
them.

We have a shortage of songs of pure praise. There are
many exhortations to praise, such as "Praise Him, Jesus,

our blessed Redeemer," but few of true adoration. Let us cherish them.

All People That on Earth Do Dwell (No. 1)   Psalm C
William Kethe, 1561
Old Hundredth (L.M.)   Louis Bourgeois
Genevan Psalter, 1551

For more than four centuries this hymn has played a leading role in the musical worship of the church, and for many more centuries before that the Hundredth Psalm, of which it is a paraphrase, was a dominant vehicle of praise.

Shakespeare mentions it in *The Merry Wives of Windsor*, Act II, Scene I: "They do no more adhere and keep place together than the Hundredth Psalm to the tune of *Greensleeves*." And Longfellow refers to it as "that grand old Puritan anthem" in *The Courtship of Miles Standish*.

It was the opening hymn at the coronation of Queen Elizabeth II, June 2, 1953, when Ralph Vaughan Williams (1872-1958) wrote a majestic setting of it that includes choral, instrumental, and congregational forces.

It was written by William Kethe, a Scottish minister, exiled to Frankfort and Geneva during the reign of Queen (Bloody) Mary. Only two words have been changed through the years: "Him serve with mirth" was originally "Him serve with fear," a much poorer translation of the Hebrew, which actually meant "gladness." The other change: "We are His flock," in the second stanza, instead of "We are His folk," came from a misunderstanding of the early spelling of "folck" (folk). Actually, the "flock" rendering suits the sheep idiom better.

This is one of the very few early hymns which has been associated with one tune during most of its life. Louis Bourgeois (c. 1500 - c. 1561) actually composed it for Psalm 134 in the *Genevan Psalter*. An altered form of the tune has been used as a setting for Bishop Thomas Ken's popular

Doxology: "Praise God from Whom All Blessings Flow" (No. 7). Another unique alteration was made for the translation of Betty Ehrenborg's Swedish hymn: "For God So Loved All the World" (No. 75).

Holy Majesty! Before Thee (No. 4)

Samuel J. Hedborn, 1812
Trans. Composite

Wachet Auf (8. 9. 8. 8. 9. 8. 6. 6. 4. 8. 8.)   Philip Nicolai, 1599

Pure worship seems to reach its loftiest level in this magnificent hymn. Coupled to its equally majestic music, it lifts the heart in almost involuntary exaltation.

Samuel Johan Hedborn (1783-1849) was born in Heda, Sweden, in deep poverty. After serving as a school teacher and a court preacher, he pastored one church until his death. During this time he wrote a considerable amount of poetry. Not many of his hymns have been translated, but they formed an important part of the "golden age" of Swedish hymnody, along with those of Wallin and Franzén

Philip Nicolai (1556-1608) was a famous and eloquent Lutheran preacher in his time who suffered considerably under Catholic persecution and, later, under the Calvinists. He is best remembered for his beautiful hymns and tunes. He wrote both text and tune of "O Morning Star! How Fair and Bright" (No. 129), and that same tune, *Frankfort*, was used for "All Hail to Thee, O Blessed Morn!" (No. 110). His *Wachet Auf* is known as "the king of the chorales" and has been incorporated into many musical compositions, including masterworks by Mendelssohn and Johann Sebastian Bach. Bach's harmonization of the tune also is used with "Now Let Every Tongue Adore Thee" (No. 576).

Now Thank We All Our God (No. 8)

Martin Rinkart, c. 1636
Trans. by Catherine Winkworth, 1858

Nun danket (6. 7. 6. 7. 6. 6. 6. 6.)   Johann Crüger, 1648

The Thirty Years' War (1618-48) was one of the most

destructive in the bloody annals of European conflicts. The prolonged years of violence and devastation were followed by famine and pestilence. Yet it is an amazing tribute to the divine source of great hymnody that Germany's greatest hymns were written during that time. It is one of the miracles of Christianity that persecution usually begets praise.

Martin Rinkart (1586-1649) was pastor during the entire period of the war. His town of Eilenburg, Saxony, was ravaged three times, and the pestilence of 1637 claimed some eight thousand lives, including all of his fellow pastors. He conducted about 4,500 funerals that year—sometimes as many as forty or fifty a day. Yet from his heart and pen poured forth one of the greatest paeans of praise of all time, often called "the Te Deum of Germany."

The text is a paraphrase of a passage in the apocryphal book Ecclesiasticus, chapter 50, verses 29 through 32: "And now let all praise God, who hath done great things, who hath glorified our days, and dealeth with us according to His loving-kindness. He giveth us the joy of our hearts, that we may find peace in Israel as in the days of yore, thus He lets His loving-kindness remain with us, and He will redeem us in our day." We are indebted to Catherine Winkworth (1829-78) for the translation, one of her many such invaluable contributions to our English hymnody.

The great hymn is most happily wed to an equally great chorale by Johann Crüger (1598-1662), one of Germany's finest and most prolific church composers. Mendelssohn incorporated it into his "Hymn of Praise," and Bach made it the basis of a cantata.

O Mighty God, When I Behold the Wonder (No. 9) Carl Boberg, 1886
Trans. by E. Gustav Johnson, 1925
O store Gud (11. 10. 11. 10. 10. 8.) Swedish folk melody

One of the most encouraging phenomena in modern

hymnody is the rapid rise to popular ascendancy of certain versions of this hymn. Popularity of a hymn does not necessarily connote merit. The masses frequently accept sentimentality for spirituality and a catchy melody for a worthy tune. But here we have a text of pure objective praise set to a charmingly simple tune that has found special favor with millions. In all candor we must admit, however, that this is not so much a triumph of popular taste as a tribute to the power of favorite personalities. For it is unquestionably the "plugging" by George Beverly Shea and other gospel singers that has stimulated this interest.

Most people, including users of Covenant hymnals, were unaware of this song until well past the mid-twentieth century, yet its author, the Rev. Carl Boberg (1859-1940), wrote it in 1886 while visiting at a beautiful country estate near Monsterås, on the southeast coast of Sweden. A sudden midday thunderstorm had burst in all its awe-inspiring fury. Just a few moments of flashing violence and it was over, the newly-washed sky aglow with the brilliant sun. The birds resumed their interrupted song and, across the bay, church bells were pealing. Pastor Boberg was driven to his knees in humble adoration of the mighty God who had created it all. He penned his praise in the nine-stanza hymn beginning with "*O store Gud, när jag den värld beskåder.*"

It was subsequently translated into German by Manfred von Glehn as "Wie gross bist Du" and in 1925 the Rev. E. Gustav Johnson of North Park College made the first English translation, the one still used in *The Hymnal.* In 1927 I. S. Prokhanoff came upon the German version and translated it into the Russian language.

The Rev. Stuart K. Hine, an English missionary, heard the Ukrainians singing the hymn and, thinking it to be a Russian folk tune, translated it and so labeled it. His version spread throughout the British Commonwealth and was introduced to American audiences at the Stony Brook

Bible Conference on Long Island in 1951. But it was not until Cliff Barrows, of the Billy Graham evangelistic team, discovered it during the famed London Crusade in Harringay Arena that the hymn was catapulted into its present orbit.

Some rather severe copyright restrictions imposed by the American entrepreneurs who published the Hine version have hampered normal progress of the hymn. Consequently, several translations and revisions have appeared, resulting in confusion for the public, which demands the popular version. The Hine translation, having been filtered through several languages, is somewhat lacking in authenticity, yet is very good, and should not be commercially restricted. The musical setting with which it is literally handcuffed is woefully unworthy, both in its poorly-voiced hymn version and in its pop-styled solo setting—replete with ukulele chords!

The original translation as found in *The Hymnal* can hardly be used congregationally, since our people have been oriented to the popularized version. Were it not for the legal restrictions, there is no doubt that a satisfactory composite text and musical setting could be devised.

The Rev. Carl Boberg was a famous preacher of his day, ranked with Waldenström, Ekman, and Palmberg of his native land. He was the successful editor of *Sanningsvittnet* and a member of the Swedish parliament. He is represented in *The Hymnal* by another fine hymn, "My Soul Now Magnifies the Lord" (No. 375), based on the ancient *Magnificat*, the song of Mary recorded in the first chapter of Luke.

Chapter Three

Times of Worship

*In God we boast all the day long, and praise thy name
for ever.*
                                        —Psalm 44:8

One of the first accounts of the activities of the early
Christian church is the letter, dated 112 A.D., from Pliny
the Younger, governor of Bithynia and Pontus, to his im-
perial master, Trajan. He reported that it was the custom
of this curious sect, called Christians, to gather before
dawn "to sing, antiphonally, hymns of praise to Christ as
God."

The day of the Christian, from early morning until evening, should be filled with praise. And there are appropriate
songs for all days and all times. Many of these are included
in this section of *The Hymnal*.

THE LORD'S DAY
*Blessed are they that dwell in thy house: they will be
still praising thee.*   —Psalm 84:4

O Day of Rest and Gladness (No. 19) Christopher Wordsworth, 1862
                                        Old German melody
Mendebras (7. 6. 7. 6. D.)   Arr. by Lowell Mason, 1839

Christopher Wordsworth (1807-85) was a brilliant man
from a distinguished English family. His uncle was the celebrated poet William Wordsworth, and his father, also
named Christopher, was master of Trinity College at Cam-

bridge. The younger Christopher also had a fourteen-year career in the academic field as headmaster of Harrow, one of England's exclusive boys' schools.

His principles were expressed in a speech made to his young charges: "It will be my earnest endeavor," he said, "to make all of you, first, Christians; secondly, gentlemen; and thirdly, scholars." He also had a term as canon of Westminster Abbey in London.

His greatest work, however, was done while in a nineteen-year pastorate in an obscure country hamlet. Here he wrote many scholarly volumes, including a commentary on the whole Bible. And here he penned his 127 hymns. This one is from his extended work called *The Holy Year*, containing hymns for all seasons of the church year.

Note the play upon the number three. The "triple light," which refers to the relationship to the Sabbath of creation, resurrection, and the gift of the Holy Spirit, is adroitly linked with the Trinity and the Tersanctus ("holy, holy, holy").

The tune, *Mendelbras*, is one of many which have come to us from purely secular sources, this being a German folk song.

MORNING HYMNS

My voice shalt thou hear in the morning, O Lord.
—Psalm 5:3

Joyful, Joyful, We Adore Thee (No. 21)   Henry van Dyke, 1907
Hymn to joy (8. 7. 8. 7. D.)   Ludwig van Beethoven, 1824

Henry van Dyke (1852-1933) was one of America's most distinguished men of letters. He was also a minister, teacher, and diplomat. He wrote this hymn during a preaching visit at Williams College. Coming down to the breakfast table, Dr. van Dyke placed a manuscript before his host, the president of the college, with the words: "Here is a hymn for you. Your mountains (the Berkshires) were my inspiration. It must be sung to the music of Beethoven's 'Hymn to Joy.' "

The work referred to was, of course, the last movement of the mighty Ninth Symphony, in which the great master combined voices and orchestra in the interpretation of Schiller's poem "Hymn to Joy."

When this monumental symphony was first produced in Vienna in 1824, the audience was so overwhelmed that the people actually shouted their delight for a period of more than ten minutes. The great composer, however, was totally deaf and oblivious both to the sound of his music and the uproar of the audience. Someone turned him around to face the now standing crowd and they, aware of his disability for the first time, were melted to tears.

Never were words more appropriately mated to music. The affinity can be understood when we read a statement about God and nature by Beethoven, who died before van Dyke was born, yet seemed to anticipate the text. "Every tree seems to speak to me of God," he said. "How happy I am to wander through the cool paths of the forest!"

EVENING HYMNS
Ye shall have a song, as in the night when a holy solemnity is kept. —Isaiah 30:29

Day Is Dying in the West (No. 30) Mary A. Lathbury, 1877
Evening Praise (Chautauqua) (7. 7. 7. 7. 4.) William F. Sherwin, 1877

The Chautauqua movement was a dominant force in the religious and cultural life of late-nineteenth-century America, and many will recall the lectures and concerts it sponsored all over the nation during the earlier decades of the twentieth century. The movement was born in the heart of Methodist Bishop John H. Vincent at an assembly on beautiful Lake Chautauqua near Jamestown, New York.

Radio, television, and modern transportation have eliminated the need for such a nation-wide institution, but its influence will continue to be felt throughout the world because of two hymns. They were both requested by Bishop Vincent, and they were both written by his two associates: Mary Artemisia Lathbury (1841-1913) and William Fiske Sherwin (1826-88).

The one, "Break Thou the Bread of Life" (No. 429), was the study hymn of the assembly and has become the best-loved hymn for Bible study the world around. The other, selected as our representative evening hymn, is one of the most inspiring of vesper songs.

George C. Stebbins, eminent gospel musician, described the occasion of the first use of this hymn:

> On Saturday evening (August 5, 1876) about two thousand people gathered on the shores of Lake Chautauqua. On the water near the shore was a boat in which were Professor Sherwin and the Stebbins brothers. About this central boat were thirty other little boats, filled with men, women, and children. . . . It was a beautiful scene and very impressive.

The text of the refrain has its roots deep in the Old Testament, in Isaiah's account of the singing of the seraphim: "Holy, holy, holy, is the Lord of hosts: the whole earth is full of his glory." This classic example of true worship was a favorite of the early Christian church, embodied in the *Tersanctus* and the *Te Deum.* It is highly significant—and rare—that such an expression should find a place in a lyric of the gospel song era.

An outstanding British hymnologist called it "one of the finest and most distinctive hymns of modern times," even though it has never caught on in England.

There is an emotional thrill in the singing of this hymn, whether in the setting of a summer camp with the roseate splendor of the setting sun reflected in the waters of a love-ly lake or in the worshipful atmosphere of the church sanc-tuary. The ascending cadences of "Wait and worship while the night/Sets her evening lamps alight" can hardly fail to lead one into the very presence of the "Lord most high."

The tempo of this song should not drag. Day is dying, but we are not singing a dirge to its demise! It is a joyful paean of praise to the Creator of it all.

OPENING HYMNS

Let us come before his presence with thanksgiving, and make a joyful noise unto him with psalms.

—Psalm 95:2

Come, Thou Fount of Every Blessing (No. 44) Robert Robinson, 1758
Nettleton (8. 7. 8. 7. D.) John Wyeth, 1812

There are at least three ways in which the study of hymn backgrounds is rewarding:

1. They are usually so interwoven with Scripture that to study them is really *Bible study.*
2. They are frequently so tied in with the personal ex-periences of the writers as to make the study *bio-graphical.*
3. To probe into the ways hymns have influenced others tends to make it a study of *personal experience.*

This hymn illustrates all three aspects in the perusal of just one phrase: "Here I raise mine Ebenezer."

We are taken back to the Old Testament account of Samuel and his gratitude to God for the miraculous deliver-ance of the Israelites from the mighty Philistines and the return of the ark of the Lord. In 1 Samuel 7:12 we read: "Then Samuel took a stone, and set it between Mizpeh and Shen, and called the name of it Ebenezer, saying, Hitherto hath the Lord helped us."

When Robert Robinson (1735-90) sang, "Here I raise

mine Ebenezer," he was erecting a spiritual marker on his life's bewildering trail. After a youth described as "wild and reckless," Robinson was converted through a sermon by George Whitefield. Further influenced by John Wesley, he took the oversight of a Calvinist Methodist church, but within two years he had transferred to an independent congregation and from thence went to a Baptist church. His "love of liberty" led him from one congregation to another, even though he was apparently successful in his ministry. Again a phrase of the hymn is suggested: "Prone to wander, Lord, I feel it."

For the experiential aspect we turn to Mrs. Frances E. Clark, co-founder with her husband of the Christian Endeavor Society. This was her favorite hymn, and one day while humming it to herself she felt impelled to "raise an Ebenezer" similar to that raised by Samuel. With stones selected from the seashore, she was joined by her family and later by other visiting Christian Endeavorers in erecting a monument to spiritual victories and their appreciation of the hymn.

The tune *Nettleton* was named for the Rev. Asahel Nettleton, well-known evangelist of the early eighteenth century. Its composer, John Wyeth (1770-1858), was a newspaper editor in Harrisburg, Pennsylvania.

CLOSING HYMNS
And when they had sung an hymn, they went out.
—Mark 14:26

Savior, Again to Thy Dear Name   John Ellerton, 1866
  We Raise (No. 57)
Ellers (10. 10. 10. 10.)   Edward J. Hopkins, 1869

It was the annual festival of the Malpas, Middlewich, and Nantwich Choral Association, and the earnest members of the assembled choirs had put their hearts in their voices during the several sessions of the festival. They had thrilled to the soaring melodies of mighty hymns and anthems, and their hearts had been warmed by the sense of God's presence. Now the time had come for the songs to cease and the joyful fellowship to come to an end. There were many moist eyes in the group as they lifted their voices in a closing hymn. It was a very special hymn, sung for the first time. It had been written for the occasion just the preceding Sunday by the Rev. John Ellerton (1826-93), vicar of one of the participating churches. He had penned it in some haste on the back of his sermon manuscript. It was a thrilling close to the choral fest. The words seemed to express the sentiments of all, just as it has on countless later occasions throughout the world.

Canon Ellerton was well-known as a preacher and writer but will be best remembered as the outstanding hymnologist of his day. He is represented in *The Hymnal* by three hymns, all in the Evening Hymns and Closing Hymns sections: "The Day Thou Gavest, Lord, Is Ended" (No. 37), "The Lord Be with Us" (No. 58), and our subject hymn.

If the author of this hymn can be said to be an expert in his field, it is no less true of the composer. Edward John Hopkins (1818-1901) was one of the finest church musicians of his time. His first position as organist was secured when he was but sixteen, the youngest in all England to hold an important organ post. He was to serve several great churches in that capacity and to stay at one London parish for 55 years. It is interesting to note that this same *Ellers* tune is used for a fine hymn in the Opening Hymn section: "Father, Again in Jesus' Name We Meet" (No. 46).

Chapter Four

The Holy Trinity

I believe in God the Father Almighty.... And in Jesus Christ, His only Son. ... I believe in the Holy Spirit.

—The Apostles' Creed

A beloved teacher of past days used to warn us, "Don't get your theology from your hymnal!" I'm sure it was good advice since *The Hymnal* is not a theology textbook and there are many poetic expressions that may serve the spirit but not the letter of sound doctrine, as well as some which may be downright questionable. Nevertheless, when the teaching is biblically correct, nowhere is theology more palatable—or retainable—than in *The Hymnal.*

Here, in four brief hymns, the almost inscrutable doctrine of the Trinity is made a reality, and something for which we can offer exulting praise.

Holy, Holy, Holy! Lord God Almighty (No. 61) Reginald Heber, 1826
Nicaea (11. 12. 12. 10.)   John B. Dykes, 1861

Here is a hymn which is the very epitome of worship, doubtless the all-American favorite opening hymn for the Sunday morning worship service. Jeremiah B. Reeves said, "Its lines suggest cathedral heights and spaces. Its spirit is that of the Hebrew prophets approaching the sovereign God." No less a poetic authority than Alfred Lord Tennyson dubbed it "the world's greatest hymn."

The text is based on both Old and New Testament references. Like one of the earliest of liturgical hymns, the *Tersanctus*, and "Day Is Dying in the West," it stems from the Isaiah account of the seraphim who cried one to another, "Holy, holy, holy is the Lord of hosts: the whole earth is full of his glory." It also has roots in the very last book of the Bible in the apocalyptic outburst of praise, "Holy, holy, holy is the Lord God Almighty, who was and is and is to come!"

This hymn was written by a most remarkable young vicar of the Church of England, Reginald Heber (1783-1826). Like Watts and several other leading hymnists, Heber was somewhat of a prodigy. As a child of seven he was translating the Socratic dialogues of Plato into English verse. While still in his teens he won prizes for both Latin and English poetry. Again like Watts, he was so dissatisfied with the Psalm-singing of his day that he wrote many hymns in the hope of replacing them in the services of the church. Most of the hymns were for various days in the church year, and many have found their way into the major hymnals and into regular use in all denominations.

The Hymnal of the Covenant Church contains only five, but they are among the best of their kind: "God, That Madest Earth and Heaven" (No. 35), "The Son of God Goes Forth to War" (No. 316), "Bread of the World in Mercy Broken" (No. 425), "From Greenland's Icy Mountains" (No. 455), and our current selection, "Holy, Holy, Holy!" (No. 61).

There is little question but that the strong tune of John Bacchus Dykes (1823-76) has had much to do with the enormous popularity of this hymn. Dykes was the outstanding hymn composer of the Victorian period and, although coming under much condemnation in our anti-Romanticism age, has never been replaced in the hearts of the people. Ten of his tunes are in *The Hymnal*. *Alford* appears three times, and *St. Agnes* is used six times.

Chapter Five

God the Father

The identification of the Persons of the Trinity is never delineated more clearly than in *The Hymnal*. As the canticles of praise fall into their various categories, we see the qualities and attributes of each. And here we have more than a mere recognition of facts; we make immediate practical use of theological truth. We actively praise God the Father for the qualities which characterize Him. We pay homage to His eternity and power, the remote attributes of His greatness; and we offer words of loving gratitude for the intimate qualities of His Fatherhood and abiding presence.

HIS ETERNITY AND POWER

O God, Our Help in Ages Past (No. 65)   Isaac Watts, 1719
St. Anne (C. M.)   William Croft, 1708

Here is an interpretation of Psalm 90, a psalm of Moses. It was originally part of "The Psalms of David Imitated," in which Isaac Watts (1674-1748) has paraphrased the entire Psalter in Christian verse. He titled the hymn "Man Frail and God Eternal," and it deals with "the vast concepts of time and eternity." It is probably the greatest of all of his six hundred hymns; indeed, it could be a contestant for the finest hymn in the English language. "It swells like the ocean," says Professor Osbert W. Warmingham; "it sobs out the grief of centuries."

The hymn was written about the middle of the eighteenth century, just before the death of Queen Anne, and the tune forever bears her name, recalling the distress in England caused by her passing. It is the great ceremonial hymn of the British empire and is used on all memorable occasions. Every day in the Strand, busiest of London's thoroughfares, this majestic tune is pealed out by the chimes of St. Clement's church.

One should read carefully verses 1, 2, 4, 12, and 17 of Psalm 90 to establish more perfectly the background of the hymn. You will note that this is not a mere metrical version of the psalm but rather an exposition—a commentary on the whole subject of *time*, which is the theme of the psalm.

A mighty text deserves a powerful tune. Such a tune is *St. Anne*, which was first intended by William Croft (1678-1727) for Psalm 42, "As Pants the Hart for Cooling Streams" (No. 396), but is much better wedded to "O God, Our Help." It is used in many fine works of music, including Bach's great "Fugue in E-flat Major," often called "St. Anne's Fugue." One of the finest choral works using this tune is Ralph Vaughan Williams' "Lord, Thou Hast Been Our Refuge," in which the original words of the psalm are superimposed upon the text of the hymn.

GOD IN NATURE

This Is My Father's World (No. 72)   Maltbie D. Babcock, 1901
Terra Beata (S. M. D.)   Franklin L. Sheppard, 1915

The writer of this hymn was a man! Even with a name like Maltbie Davenport Babcock and a predilection for writing poetry, there was never any question about his manliness. From his early boyhood days he was a natural leader in athletics.

And he had a forceful personality to match. One day while walking to the seminary where he was studying for the ministry, he saw a bully picking on a smaller boy. Putting down his briefcase, Maltbie Babcock seized the big fellow by the nape of the neck and the seat of his trousers and tossed him over the fence.

All boys should read the story of this man among men who didn't think it sissy to play the piano, organ, and violin; and who unashamedly loved Christ and His church.

Babcock was born in 1858 in Syracuse, New York, and died just forty-three years later in Naples, Italy, while on a Mediterranean tour. During that rather short career he lived life at a high dynamic level, making an imprint for good upon all whom he touched. Eighteen months before he died, he had succeeded the famed Dr. Henry van Dyke as pastor of the historic Brick Presbyterian Church in New York City.

While a pastor in Lockport, New York, Dr. Babcock was in the habit of taking morning walks to the top of a hill north of town where he had a full view of Lake Ontario and the surrounding country. He used to announce, "I'm going out to see my Father's world."

After his death, his wife Katherine published a volume of her husband's poems, including this sixteen-stanza hymn. Mr. Franklin Laurence Sheppard (1852-1930), a Baltimore businessman and a member of Dr. Babcock's congregation, read the poem and conceived the tune which is now so closely associated with the hymn. Mr. Sheppard was reluctant to claim authorship, feeling that it might have been a song he had heard elsewhere. Thus the tune is still listed in some books as an "Old English Melody." Its source has never been found, and there is no longer any reason to doubt its originality.

That this hymn is more than a poem in praise of nature is understood when one reads some lines of prose by Dr. Babcock: "This is the best possible world for one who is called according to God's purpose. God knows why we are here and has told us—to learn and to do—for discipline and duty. Can we imagine a world better fitted for those ends than this one? Let us not look too much out of the schoolroom windows, or too impatiently at the clock. When God's time for us comes, well and good. Till then, this world is best for us, and we must make the most of it and do our best for it."

GOD'S LOVE AND FATHERHOOD

I Greet Thee, Who My Sure Redeemer Art (No. 80) John Calvin, 1545
Toulon (10. 10. 10. 10.)   Derived from Old 124th
                                        "Genevan Psalter," 1551

John Calvin (1509-64) was one of the most influential theologians of all time, yet this hymn, the only one by him to be found in our modern repertory, is in no way a polemic but one of the most sublime salutations to the Savior ever penned.

The very fact that Calvin should have written a hymn is remarkable, since he was a strong advocate of the exclusive use of psalm-singing by his followers, a practice still observed by some Calvinistic church groups. During his enforced exile in Geneva, he caused to be compiled the *Genevan Psalter*, possibly the most famous book of praise ever produced by the Christian church.

He is said to have frowned upon the German chorale, considering it too florid for the sanctuary, yet he was so much impressed with the singing of the Lutherans in Strassburg that he wrote, "The singing has such force and vigor as to stir up and inflame the hearts of men to invoke and praise God with zeal most passionate and burning."

The psalm-singing at Geneva was probably less forceful, but its fervency is attested by a firsthand account written by an English visitor: "A most interesting sight is offered in the city on week days, when the hour for service approaches. As soon as the first sound of the bell is heard, all shops are closed, conversation ceases, business is put aside, and from all parts people hasten to the nearest church. Arrived there, each one draws from his pocket a small book which contains some psalms with meter, and then the congregation sings before and after the sermon, while everyone testifies how great consolation is derived from this custom."

The tune *Toulon* is an adaptation of one used four centuries ago as the musical setting for Psalm 124. It is a unique and powerful tune, used elsewhere in *The Hymnal* with "God of the Nations" (No. 495) and "God of the Prophets" (No. 557).

GOD'S ABIDING PRESENCE

God Moves in a Mysterious Way (No. 96)   William Cowper, 1774
Dundee (C. M.)   Scottish Psalter, 1615

For those who relish dramatic stories served up with their hymn studies, here is a veritable gourmet's delight. Several such tales, probably apocryphal, are told concerning this superb hymn. All concern the deep melancholy of this great hymnist, William Cowper (1731-1800), and his proneness toward suicide attempts. In one story he calls for a carriage and directs the driver to a bridge on the river Ouse, where he intended to drown himself. The driver gets his directions confused and, after driving about for some time, returns the poet to his home. A variation of this account has the presence of a porter and low tide as the intervening circumstances. There are other versions, all of which point up the incipient insanity of this brilliant but unhappy man. It is quite probable that some such incident prompted the writing of this hymn. The fact that these mental lapses often brought about the writing of inspiring hymns is in itself proof enough of the truth of this powerful text: "God moves in a mysterious way, His wonders to perform."

Cowper was one of the very few great poets who were also great hymn writers. Some would call him the most popular poet of his generation. Haeussler describes him as "the connecting link between the classicists represented by Pope, and the naturalists typified by Burns and Wordsworth." His mother, who died when he was six, was a descendant of John Donne, the English poet, and his father was court chaplain to George II. Young William studied law but was never able to practice because of an innate fear. Some unhappy experiences while at boarding school had contributed to this fear which ultimately led to his periods of mental illness. During the intervals between these attacks he was most lucid, possessing a masterful gift of expression combined with a deep spiritual insight.

For some time he made his home with the Reverend Morley Unwin and his family. After Mr. Unwin's death in 1767, they moved to Olney, where Cowper made the friendship of John Newton, curate of the church there. Together Newton and Cowper published the *Olney Hymns* in 1779, the first great hymnal of the Anglican Church.

William Cowper is well represented in all hymnals. Notwithstanding the frequent depression of the writer, his hymns are rarely gloomy but are filled with vivid imagery born of the poet's skill and rich spiritual depth. Outstanding are "The Spirit Breathes Upon the Word" (No. 221), with its deathless lines: "A glory gilds the sacred page,/ Majestic like the sun;/It gives a light to every age;/It gives, but borrows none"; the controversial "There Is a Fountain Filled with Blood" (No. 257), "Jesus, Where'er Thy People Meet" (No. 302), and "O for a Closer Walk with God" (No. 401).

The tune *Dundee* is one of the fine Psalm tunes to come out of Scotland during the seventeenth century.

He Leadeth Me! O Blessed Thought!
(No. 98)
He Leadeth Me (L. M. with refrain)

Joseph H. Gilmore, 1862

William B. Bradbury, 1864

When visiting the city of Philadelphia, one usually takes in the many historic shrines of early Americana. One that the guides will seldom point out is of special interest to hymn lovers. It is a rather insignificant weathered bronze tablet on a building at the corner of Broad and Arch, one of the city's busiest intersections. If you can avoid being trampled by the hurrying crowds, you should pause and read it.

" 'He Leadeth Me,' sung throughout the world, was written by the Reverend Dr. Joseph H. Gilmore, a son of a Governor of New Hampshire, in the home of Deacon Wattson, immediately after preaching in the First Baptist Church, Northwest Corner Broad and Arch Streets, on the 26th day of March, 1862. The church and Deacon Wattson's home stood on the ground upon which this building is erected. The United Gas Improvement Company, in recognition of the beauty and fame of the Hymn, and in remembrance of its distinguished author, makes this permanent record on the first day of June, 1926."

A few more details complete the interesting story. Dr. Gilmore was not the pastor of the church, but was a recent theological graduate temporarily supplying the pulpit. It was the midweek service, and he was giving an exposition of Psalm 23, one which he had presented several times before. But on this occasion he could get no farther than the words "He leadeth me."

After the service Dr. and Mrs. Gilmore went to Deacon Wattson's home next door, where they and several friends visited over some refreshments. "During the conversation," recounted Dr. Gilmore, "the blessedness of God's leadership so grew upon me that I took out my pencil, wrote the hymn just as it stands today, handed it to my wife, and thought no more about it."

If the story had ended there, we would not be telling it today. There is a sequel. Three years later when Dr. Gilmore was in Rochester, New York, to preach at the Second Baptist Church of the city, he was leafing through the unfamiliar hymnal prior to the start of the service. He was startled to see there his forgotten poem, together with his name and a musical setting by William B. Bradbury! His wife had sent the verses to a Boston paper, *The Watchman and Reflector*, where it had been seen by Bradbury (1816-68), a prolific composer and compiler of gospel songs.

The song has found its way into many languages and is sung the world around. Servicemen during World War II found it to be a popular hymn among the primitive Polynesians in the South Pacific. And in Sweden several generations have been singing: *Han leder mig! Han leder mig! Ja, med sin hand han leder mig!*

Chapter Six

Jesus Christ the Lord

... and there were great voices in heaven, saying, "The kingdoms of this world are become the kingdoms of our Lord, and of his Christ." —Revelation 11:15

Our tributes of praise to the second Person of the Trinity are closely associated with the events of His life. Through our hymns we join the angels and shepherds in heralding His birth; we actively participate in the events leading to His death and resurrection; and we stand with the disciples as with upturned faces they watch His ascension and anticipate His reappearing.

HIS ADVENT

In the church calendar, Advent is a four-Sunday season of preparing for Christmas. Traditionally, there is the symbolical use of the Palm Sunday entrance of our Lord into Jerusalem—a fact which makes several of the hymns in this division interchangeable with the section on "His Triumphal Entry." There are also foreshadowings of His second advent in the songs and lessons of this period.

Lift Up Your Heads, Ye Mighty Gates (No. 103) Georg Weissel, 1641
Trans. by Catherine Winkworth, 1855
Truro (L. M.)   Thomas Williams' "Psalmodia Evangelica," 1789

This excellent Advent hymn, based on Psalm 24:7-10,

dates to the early seventeenth century for its German origin. Georg Weissel (1590-1635) was one of the most important of the early Prussian hymnists, even though he wrote but twenty hymns. They became standard for the various festivals of the church year, and three have been translated into English by that artist among translators, Catherine Winkworth (1829-78).

A special tribute should be paid to Miss Winkworth and other translators for their worthy contribution to hymnody. Without their dedicated work many great hymns would be confined to one tongue. The translation of a hymn involves more than the faithful rendering of the meaning from one language to another, although it must include that. Good hymnic poetry is more than thoughts and ideas. There must be that touch of lyrical artistry that captures the thought and the imagination as well. The quality that made it good poetry in the original language must somehow be transported across the lingual barrier. This Catherine Winkworth did with consummate skill. Her success is attested by the number of her translations appearing in the standard hymnals. Eight are to be found in the Covenant collection.

The tune, *Truro*, is by an unknown composer, first appearing in the collection of psalm and hymn tunes compiled by Thomas Williams. This is the only extant tune from this volume, and is anonymous.

HIS BIRTH

Our hymnody is so rich in its Christmas traditions that one finds it extremely difficult to stay within the confines allotted to this division. Yet, numerous as are the hymns on the birth of Christ, there is need for their active promotion. Confined to but one brief period of the year, there is a possibility that some may be used so infrequently as to become extinct. Also, they are currently under fire as being unconstitutional in their use outside the church and as too specific in their theology for compatibility with modern changing concepts. If one objects to scriptural teachings about the nativity, such fears are not unfounded. Consider but a few phrases from some of the best-known Christmas songs: "Offspring of a virgin's womb," "incarnate Deity," "born to give them second birth," "Word of the Father now in flesh appearing," "Cast out our sin . . . be born in us to-day." Yes, although our carols abound in vague references to a baby in a manger, angels, shepherds, and the like, there are also many with foreshadowings of the cross and salvation's complete story. Note should be made of the fact that, in the church calendar, Christmas begins on December 25 and continues for twelve days thereafter.

All Hail to Thee, O Blessed Morn! (No. 110) Johan Olof Wallin, 1819
Trans. by Ernst W. Olson (1870-1958)
Frankfort (Irregular) Philip Nicolai, 1599

For more than a century there has been but one musical greeting to the dawn of Christmas Day in the churches of Sweden. The sanctuaries have reverberated uniformly with the strains of *Var hälsad, sköna morgonstund*. And the Swedish-oriented assemblies in America and elsewhere have quite generally followed suit.

It is a practice which other congregations could copy with profit. Here is a rare jewel of lyric beauty from the pen of one of Christendom's greatest hymnists set to the majestic cadences of "the Queen of the Chorales." And unlike most of Wallin's hundreds of Swedish hymns, this hymn has a very adequate translation into English.

It was Henry Wadsworth Longfellow who introduced Johan Olof Wallin (1779-1838) to the English-speaking world. "And with one voice," reads his translation of a Swedish poem by Tegnér, "chimed in the congregation, and sang an anthem immortal of the sublime Wallin, of David's harp in the Northland."

"David's harp in the Northland" was the pen of Wallin in truth. The great Swedish *Psalmbook (Den Svenska Psalmboken)* of 1819, the dominant hymnal of the nation for more than a hundred years, was largely the work of this one man. No less than 342 of the 500 hymns in the collection were written, revised, or translated by Wallin.

One catches a glimpse of his governing ideals in Wallin's statement that "a new hymn, aside from the spiritual considerations, which must not be compromised in any way, should be so correct, simple, and lyrical in form that after the lapse of a hundred years a father may be able to say to his son, 'Read the Psalmbook, my boy, and you will learn your mother tongue!' "

The aura of spiritual and literary excellence has clung to his hymns even through the crucible of translation. Consider those found in *The Hymnal:* the salute to the dawn, "Again Thy Glorious Sun Doth Rise" (No. 22); the Advent hymns, "Jerusalem, Lift Up Thy Voice" (No. 101) and "O Bride of Christ, Rejoice" (No. 104); and the simple eloquence of such prayers as "Jesus, Lord and Precious Savior" (No. 386) and "Watch, My Soul, and Pray" (No. 408).

The hymns of Wallin are characteristically stately, but they are never somber and should never drag. The mighty chorale of Philip Nicolai (he also wrote "the King of Chorales," discussed in chapter two) is symbolical of the Wallin text and of the man, the man who could call out with his dying breath, "My Lord, I am coming! My country, my King, my God!"

Thou Didst Leave Thy Throne (No. 126) Emily E. Steele Elliot, 1864
Margaret (Irregular)   Timothy R. Matthews, 1876

As with a number of the hymns of the nativity, this

hymn goes far beyond the birth to deal with the life and ministry of our Lord and even to speak of the necessity of heart-acceptance of Christ and of His coming in glory. It is in reality a sermon exposition of a text found in Luke 2:7, "There was no room for them in the inn."

Miss Emily Elizabeth Steele Elliot (1836-97) wrote the hymn for the choir and children of St. Mark's church in Brighton, England, where her father, the Rev. Edward B. Elliot, was rector. She wrote most of her hymns for specific purposes in her church or for patients in hospitals and infirmaries with whom she spent much of her time and energy. One collection of hymns planned for the latter group was titled *Under the Pillow.*

Margaret was written for the poem by Timothy Richard Matthews (1826-1910), one of Britain's most prominent organists, who was also a clergyman and a composer.

HIS EPIPHANY

In the Western church, this season is devoted to the progressive revelation of Jesus as true God. Epiphany Day itself, occurring on January 6, commemorates the visit of the Magi to the infant Jesus. This was probably more than a year after His birth. Several inaccuracies are associated with this story, some being reflected in our hymns. We do not know that the Magi were three in number, or that they were kings, and we are not given their names. We do know that the occasion was subsequent to the visit of the shepherds to the stable and that it should be celebrated after the Christmas season. The principal message of Epiphany concerns the manifestation of Christ to the Gentiles. It is an excellent time for a missionary emphasis.

As with Gladness Men of Old (No. 130)   William C. Dix, 1861
Dix (7. 7. 7. 7. 7. 7.)   Conrad Kocher, 1838

William Chatterton Dix (1837-98) was one of a number

of laymen who contributed to *The Hymnal*. Born at Bristol, England, the son of a surgeon, he went into the insurance business and became general manager of a company in Glasgow. His desire to serve his God above and beyond the world of commerce plunged him into literary and language study. He learned Greek and Ethiopian, translating hymns from those languages. He authored some forty hymns, among them being the popular song of the nativity, "What Child Is This?" (No. 127), set to the lovely *Greensleeves* tune; and the comforting "Come unto Me, Ye Weary" (No. 350) with its equally beautiful Welsh melody.

The tune was for a time credited to the author of the text, but Mr. Dix disavowed it quite vehemently, saying he disliked the music. It has nevertheless continued to be associated with this hymn, even to the extent of being called *Dix*. Conrad Kocher (1786-1872), an outstanding organist and church musician of Stuttgart, Germany, wrote the music for a German text. It has proven to be one of our finest hymn tunes, used in *The Hymnal* three times.

HIS LIFE AND MINISTRY

Hymn writers have been so enchanted by the major events in the life of our Lord as to have neglected the years of His ministry on earth. One could hope to see more hymns based on His miracles and His many divine utterances, relating them to our life and times. This is one of the gaps which become evident when a search is made for hymns suitable for various sermon texts. The five hymns included in this section are in the nature of tributes to the person of our Lord.

Strong Son of God, Immortal Love (No. 136) Alfred Tennyson, 1850
St. Crispin (L. M.)   George J. Elvey, 1862

Alfred Tennyson (1809-92) was one of several great

poets and composers who found their way into *The Hymnal* almost by accident. He wrote no hymns as such, but lines from some of his poems have been extracted and used, including the well-known "Sunset and Evening Star" and "Ring Out, Wild Bells."

Certainly the most sublime and inspiring of his poem excerpts, and the only one in *The Hymnal,* is this portrait of the Lord Jesus. Some scriptural bases for the truths contained in this affirmation of faith are: "Whom having not seen, ye love; in whom, though now ye see him not, yet believing, ye rejoice with joy unspeakable and full of glory" (1 Peter 1:8); "Now faith is the substance of things hoped for, the evidence of things not seen" (Hebrews 11:1); and Peter's firm declaration, "Thou art the Christ, the Son of the living God" (Matthew 16:16).

Lord Tennyson had his times of doubting and moments of seeming heterodoxy, but in his "In Memoriam," from which this hymn is taken, he seemed to fight through the theological and scientific confusion of his day to a genuine and abiding faith. For all his erudition, his was a simple trust in Christ. "What the sun is to that flower, that," he once said, "Jesus Christ is to my soul."

The *St. Crispin* tune was composed by George Job Elvey (1816-93) for the hymn "Just as I Am, Without One Plea." Elvey, a great organist-composer in his day, was not a prolific composer of hymn tunes. Those that we have, however, are very strong and singable, as exemplified by his *Diademata,* used with "Crown Him with Many Crowns" (No. 168); and *St. George's Windsor,* the setting for "Come, Ye Thankful People, Come" (No. 541).

HIS TRIUMPHAL ENTRY

Some very stately and moving hymns have centered on the Palm Sunday theme. In them, along with the pomp and majesty, is the sombre foreboding of the passion events to take place later in the Holy Week. Most of the hymns listed in the Advent section are also applicable here.

All Glory, Laud, and Honor (No. 137) Theodulph of Orleans (c. 820)
Trans. by John M. Neale, 1854
St. Theodulph (7. 6. 7. 6. D.) Melchior Teschner, 1615

A cluster of legends has gathered about this hymn during the eleven centuries of its use, none more fascinating than that of its origin. Theodulph of Orleans (760-821) was a native of Italy, brought to France by Charlemagne and made Bishop of Orleans. He fell into disfavor under Charlemagne's successor, Louis I—called "the Pious"—and was banished to a cloister in Angers. It was during this imprisonment that he wrote the seventy-eight line hymn, *"Gloria, Laus et Honor."* It is said that he was singing the hymn in his cell on Palm Sunday, 821, when the king passed by. So moved was King Louis, runs the tale, that he ordered the Bishop's release.

The translation is by John Mason Neale (1818-66), who did more than anyone to make available to the English-speaking world the rich treasures of Greek and Latin hymnody. The original poem has been reduced to twenty-four lines for our present use. The omission of one of the stanzas can be considered fortunate. It read: "Be Thou, O Lord, the rider,/And we the little ass,/That to God's holy city/Together we may pass." *The Hymnal* contains ten of Dr. Neale's translations.

Melchior Teschner (1584-1635) was one of the best of the early Lutheran composers, remembered today by this one chorale. It is one of the noblest of the seventeenth-century tunes and has been given numerous choral and instrumental settings, notably that by J. S. Bach in his "Passion according to St. John."

HIS PASSION

The hymns on the subject of the passion of our Lord are probably the greatest group of lyrics in Christian hymnlore; this is as it should be, for this is the focal point in our faith. It is to be noted that these are not laments for a fallen hero. Not funeral dirges, but canticles of praise for a completed redemptive work. Expressions of grief at the suffering of our Friend and Brother, yes, but always the note of triumph at the purposeful death of our Savior and Lord. Needless to say, the hymns of the atonement are not confined to this section of *The Hymnal*. This is the theme that pervades the entire volume.

Come to Calvary's Holy Mountain (No. 143) James Montgomery, 1819
Naar mit øie, traet af møie Ludvig M. Lindeman (1812-87)
(8. 7. 8. 7. 7. 7.) Consolation

Of James Montgomery (1771-1854) Julian, the hymnologist, said: "His knowledge of Holy Scripture was most extensive. His devotional spirit was of the holiest type. With the faith of a strong man he united the beauty and simplicity of a child. Richly poetic without exuberance, dogmatic without uncharitableness, tender without sentimentality, elaborate without diffusiveness, richly musical without apparent effort, he has bequeathed to the church wealth which could only have come from true genius and a sanctified heart."

The Hymnal is enriched by thirteen hymns from the pen of this talented Scot who died a missionary to the West Indies. All of them are generously laced with scriptural allusions and references. Take time to read Zechariah 13:1, John 4:14, 2 Kings 5:13, Hebrews 10:22, and 1 John 1:7, and you will thrill at the intricate weaving of Holy Writ into the texture of this hymn.

Ludvig Mathias Lindeman was called "the singer who

taught the Norwegian people to sing." Acquaintance with this hymn should cause us to agree with Professor John Dahle when he said, "Lindeman's tunes breathe a spirit of deep religious fervor, refreshing vigor, and partake of the character of the folk-song."

O Sacred Head, Now Wounded   Ascribed to Bernard of Clairvaux
(No. 151)   (1091-1153)
Trans. (into German) Paul Gerhardt, 1656
Trans. (from the German) James W. Alexander, 1830
Passion Chorale (7. 6. 7. 6. D.)   Hans Leo Hassler, 1601
Har. by Johann Sebastian Bach, 1729

It took at least five men and eight centuries to produce this sublime hymn as we have it today. I use the phrase "at least" since the tune arranged by Hassler was originally a German folksong and must have involved other musicians before it reached the status of a hymn tune.

The original text was from a most remarkable work by an even more remarkable man. Possibly no preacher in all history exerted a more profound influence over his age than did Bernard of Clairvaux, a devout Cistercian monk, called by Luther the holiest man of his time. Kings and emperors sought him out for counsel. Entire towns were converted through his ministry. Yet he was among the humblest of men, living in abject poverty in the monastery he founded in France.

Alone in his narrow cell, Bernard envisioned the crucified Savior and penned a rapturous ode to "the sacred members of Christ suffering and hanging on the cross." There were seven parts to the hymn, addressed to the head, hands, feet, knees, breast, side, and heart of Jesus. Each part comprised five stanzas of ten lines each. The only portion of this 350-line poem in current use is that addressed to the "sacred head."

Paul Gerhardt (1607-76), who translated the hymn into

German, is considered the greatest of German hymn writers. It is usual for hymns to lose something in translation. This is a noteworthy exception. One authority states: "Bernard's original is powerful and searching, but Gerhardt's hymn is still more powerful and profound, as redrawn from the deeper spring of evangelical Lutheran, scriptural knowledge, and fervency of faith."

James Waddell Alexander (1804-59), an eminent nineteenth-century Presbyterian minister, is responsible for the excellent English version.

When one adds to this illustrious tradition the nobility of the *Passion Chorale* musical setting, it is easy to account for the unique place this hymn holds. Johann Sebastian Bach was partial to this chorale by the great Baroque composer, Hans Leo Hassler (1564-1612), using it five times in his *St. Matthew Passion*.

This is a solemn hymn but not a doleful one. It incorporates not only the substitutionary suffering of the Savior but also our grateful and joyous response. Its spirit is typical of its author, the saintly Bernard, who once said: "Jesus is honey to the lips, in the ear melody, in the heart joy. Medicine also is that name. Is any sad? Let Jesus come into his heart, and thence leap to his tongue!"

HIS RESURRECTION

The very essence of Christianity is Easter, and Christian hymnody reaches its pinnacle in expressing its exultant message. It is unfortunate that general usage is confined to one day. Actually, the church calendar assigns forty days to the celebration of Easter, and the construction of the Christian week designates every first day as a commemoration of the resurrection. Yet local tradition is so strong that only rarely will we sing Easter songs on any day but Easter.

The Day of Resurrection (No. 163) John of Damascus (8th Century)
Trans. by John M. Neale, 1862

Lancashire (7. 6. 7. 6. D.)   Henry Smart, 1836

It is Easter morning in the ancient city of Athens. The report of a cannon at the stroke of midnight has announced it to the thousands of people who have waited in silence for this moment.

The archbishop raises a cross and proclaims in a loud voice: *"Christos anesti!"* "Christ is risen!" The great multitude takes up the cry, "He is risen indeed!" as each worshiper lights a taper and holds it aloft.

The roll of drums is heard in all the streets, followed by the blare of many bands, the boom of cannons, and the blaze of ascending rockets. There are ecstatic shouts of joy, embracing, and the clasping of hands as each one relives the thrilling realization of the glorious truth of the resurrection.

Then is begun the massive processional to the church for a continuation of the celebration. And the hymn they are chanting as they approach the house of God is "The Day of Resurrection."

Thus for more than twelve centuries has Easter been greeted in the Greek Church. The excitement of the occasion seems not to lessen through the years of re-enactment, nor does the luster of the resurrection story become dim.

This traditional hymn is one of several noble canticles to come from the famous monastery of Mar Saba located in a desert spot of Judea overlooking the Dead Sea.

In this cloistered wilderness home lived John of Damascus in the early eighth century. He had forsaken the world and a brilliant career, taking with him his ten-year-old nephew, Stephen. Many hymns were written in the course of their monastic lives, only a few of which have found their way into our hymnals. Stephen gave us "Art Thou Weary, Art Thou Languid?" and John two great Easter hymns: "The Day of Resurrection" and "Come, Ye Faithful, Raise the Strain" (No. 157).

Again we are indebted to John Mason Neale (see page 46) for the English version.

Lancashire was composed by Henry Smart (1813-79) for "From Greenland's Icy Mountains" and was first sung at a festival celebrating the tercentenary of the Reformation. It is now closely associated with "Lead On, O King Eternal" and "The Day of Resurrection." It is used four times in *The Hymnal.*

Smart was an outstanding church musician of his day. He designed and built a number of the fine organs of England. His best-known hymn tunes, besides *Lancashire*, are *Regent Square* ("Angels from the Realms of Glory") and *Pilgrims* ("Hark, Hark My Soul").

HIS ASCENSION AND REIGN

Ascension Day, occurring forty days after Easter, is not uniformly recognized by nonliturgical churches. It never falls on Sunday, but can be celebrated on the following Sunday. It marks the close of the Easter period and the preparation for Pentecost Sunday. Its hymns, which are not numerous, emphasize the glory and majesty of the ascended Lord and are appropriate for any time of the year. The most clearly appropriate in *The Hymnal* are Kelly's "Look, Ye Saints, the Sight is Glorious" (No. 170) and Wordsworth's "See the Conqueror Mounts in Triumph" (No. 172).

All Hail the Power of Jesus' Name (No. 166) Edward Perronet, 1779
Stanza 4 added by John Rippon, 1787
Coronation (C. M.) Oliver Holden, 1793

The evangelistic ministry of John Wesley was punctuated by much mob violence. His detailed diary abounds in accounts of turbulence such as took place at Bolton, England, when an angry throng besieged the house in which he was staying. "My good friend," Wesley wrote, "ventured out of the house and was thrown down and rolled in mud and mire."

"My good friend" in this case was one Edward Perronet (1726-92), preacher, author, and poet, whose claim to lasting fame rests on this magnificent hymn.

Friend though he was, Perronet refused to preach in the presence of the great Wesley. One day, without notice, Wesley announced that the young man would occupy the pulpit the following day. Perronet said nothing, but when he mounted the rostrum he explained that he had not consented to preach. "However," he added, "I will deliver the greatest sermon that has ever been preached on earth!" He then read the Sermon on the Mount from the Bible and sat down without comment.

Based on Revelation 19, "On his head were many crowns; . . . and on his vesture and on his thigh a name written, KING OF KINGS AND LORD OF LORDS," this is one of the best-known hymns in the world, having been translated into almost every known language. Many stories cluster about its history, one of the most remarkable involving the saving of a life. A missionary to India, the Rev. E. P. Scott, was pioneering in an area where the gospel had never been preached. He had been waylaid by a murderous band of tribesmen who were closing in on him with spears. On impulse, the missionary took his violin out of his luggage and, closing his eyes, started to play the hymn "All Hail the Power of Jesus' Name." He played the tune three times, and when he reached the stanza which would have been "Let ev'ry kindred, ev'ry tribe," he opened his eyes and found they had dropped their spears and some had been moved to tears! He remained with the tribe for two and a half years, and when he was obliged to return to

America, many of his converts walked over forty miles with him, begging him to stay with them. Abruptly, he turned back and stayed, remaining until his death with the people whom the Spirit of God had conquered through the use of a simple hymn-tune.

Three fine tunes are currently in use with this hymn: *Miles Lane*, which is the most popular in Britain, by William Shrubsole, Perronet's friend; the festive *Diadem*, frequently used by choirs, by James Ellor, a Lancashire hatter; and *Coronation*, best-known in America and the only one in *The Hymnal*, composed by Oliver Holden (1765-1844), a New England carpenter.

Perronet's classic last words give insight to the spirit of the man: "Glory to God in the height of His divinity! Glory to God in the depth of His humanity! Glory to God in His all-sufficiency! Into His hand I commend my spirit."

HIS COMING IN GLORY

All of the events in the life of our Lord are in the past, save one: His promised return in power and glory. The believer sings of the other events in retrospect; of this Second Advent he sings in joyous anticipation.

Mine Eyes Have Seen the Glory (No. 178)   Julia Ward Howe, 1861
Battle Hymn of the Republic   John William Steffe (c. 1852)
    (15. 15. 15. 6. with refrain)

When the late Sir Winston Churchill made specific requests regarding his funeral arrangements, he chose two hymns to be used. The one selection, "O God, Our Help in Ages Past" (No. 65), was not surprising, but the other choice was a bit more unexpected. This outstanding "man of the century," this Briton among Britons, chose as one of his two favorite hymns a distinctively American song, the "Battle Hymn of the Republic"! The designation was, we are told, in deference to his American-born mother and to his honorary United States citizenship.

Here is a song of the strangest origin and of the most persistent popularity. Sometimes denounced as "doggerel poetry set to a jig tune," it has also been glorified as "the marching hymn of a nation." It speaks of a doctrine often disputed by the major denominations, yet it could be sung by memory by almost any congregation in the land. It has one of the simplest of tunes and employs but three chords throughout. Its rhythmic pattern is monotonously repetitious. Yet it has been incorporated into complex musical scores and performed by great musical organizations. Most current hymnals exclude it, yet its message and melody continue to thrill and bless. What is the story of this strange and immortal song?

John William Steffe of Richmond, Virginia, wrote a camp meeting song in 1852 called "Say, Brothers, Will You Meet Us?" A few years later it became a Civil War song, a rather grisly but powerful bit of propaganda called "John Brown's Body."

This was the song sung by the soldiers marching through the streets of Washington, D. C., one day in the fall of 1861. Julia Ward Howe (1819-1910), brilliant Boston writer; her husband, a noted physician; and their pastor, the Rev. James F. Clarke, were visiting the nation's capital and were painfully aware of the tumultuous days. At the singing of "John Brown's Body" Pastor Clarke turned to Mrs. Howe with the remark, "Why don't you write some good words to that stirring tune?" "I have often prayed that I might," was her reply.

It was in the gray dawn of the next morning that Mrs. Howe lay awake in her room in the Willard Hotel and found the long lines of the poem forming themselves in her mind. The now-famous words were quickly put on paper and soon published in the *Atlantic Monthly*, from which the hymn literally leaped into public favor.

Great as this hymn is in its nationalistic concepts, one wonders how often it is thought of as a purveyor of the truth of "Christ's Coming in Glory." In this it is probably typical of many familiar texts which are sung without full appreciation of their meaning.

PRAISE TO CHRIST THE LORD

Our praise to the Lord Jesus Christ has special characteristics not found in general praise to the Trinity or to God the Father. His incarnation as a man, His identification with us in His death, His intercessory activities at the right hand of God for us—all these tend to encourage an intimate affinity which is expressed by many hymns and gospel songs.

Can We Forbear to Sing (No. 189) Joseph Swain (1761-96)
Wennerberg (S. M.) Gunnar Wennerberg (1817-1901)

This hymn might fall into the category of what Armin Haeussler, the great contemporary hymnologist, calls "conversational hymns" except that the answers to the questions posed by the singer are all understood rather than expressed. It is actually an apologetic of praise, setting forth incontrovertible reasons which should extract a song from the most mute of worshipers.

The Rev. Joseph Swain had started a career as an engraver when he was converted and led into the ministry through contact with Dr. John Rippon, pastor for sixty-three years of the famed Carter Lane Church in London. Dr. Rippon, one of the best hymnologists of his time, also encouraged Swain in the writing of hymns. "Can We Forbear" is found in few American hymnals. Better known is his "O Thou, in Whose Presence My Soul Takes Delight," which has become part of early American folklore.

The musical setting is admirably suited to the text, although not expressly written for it. It is one of the few available hymn tunes by the Swedish composer Wennerberg. This popular poet and musician was a member of the Swedish legislature and was entirely self-taught in music. His choral compositions, many of them untranslated from the Swedish language, have long been popular with choirs in his own country, particularly his *"Davids Psalmer."*

Chapter Seven

The Holy Spirit

Build yourselves up on your most holy faith; pray in the Holy Spirit.
—Jude 20

We have been told that, technically, we do not pray to the Holy Spirit. We pray *to* God the Father, *through* Jesus Christ, *by* the Holy Spirit. This is both logical and theological, but not completely satisfying. There is an intimacy to be experienced with God the Holy Spirit not shared by the other persons of the Godhead. We worship and adore God the Father, the Creator of all things. We praise Jesus Christ the Son, by whom God made Himself known and through whom we have redemption. But it is God the Holy Spirit who enlightens us regarding these and other truths. It is He who draws us and indwells and gives us power to live the Christian life. We have something special to say to Him in our prayers and in our hymns. The various hymns in this section identify Him as Light, Fire, Wind, a Dove, the Breath of God, and the Comforter. But above and beyond the metaphorical mysteries, He is God becoming involved with us in all the affairs of our daily lives, and we must become dynamically involved with Him.

Breathe on Me, Breath of God (No. 203)   Edwin Hatch, 1886
Swabia (S. M.)   Johann Martin Spiess (1715-c. 1766)

Edwin Hatch (1835-89) was one of the most brilliant of

British theologians and classical scholars. He taught at Oxford for many years and wrote copiously on a variety of subjects. Yet today, less than a century later, his erudite works are forgotten. He is remembered solely for this simple hymn. And this is as it should be, for, despite his scholarly attainments, Dr. Hatch is said by a biographer to have possessed a faith "as simple and unaffected as a child's."

This hymn has been used with many musical settings, predominantly *Trentham* (No. 89). The *Swabia* usage is somewhat unique, shared only by the Episcopal *Hymnal* of 1940, in which a choice is offered between this and a contemporary tune, *Nova Vita*.

Swabia is a most excellent hymn tune, evincing a vitality properly related to the dynamic Spirit of God, filling "with life anew." It is an arrangement by W. H. Havergal (1793-1870), father of Frances Ridley Havergal, of a chorale by Johann Martin Spiess. Spiess was an organist-director in Heidelberg, compiler of a large *choralbuch* of Genevan psalm tunes and German chorales.

Holy Ghost, with Light Divine (No. 208)   Andrew Reed, 1817
Mercy (7. 7. 7. 7.)   Arr. from Louis M. Gottschalk, 1867

Most hymnals exhibit a weeful weakness in the area of hymns on the Holy Spirit. *The Hymnal* of the Covenant Church contains 10, contrasted with 35 hymns on God the Father and 102 on Jesus Christ. There are a number of logical reasons for this, but certainly the hazy, impersonal approach of the average Christian to the Third Person of the Trinity must be a contributory factor. The standard image of the Holy Spirit has not challenged hymn writers to any great extent.

When a writer has assayed to inscribe a lyric to the Holy Spirit, it has usually resulted in an ode of quiet restraint, if not downright lugubrious in nature. To illustrate the latter type, we would apologetically point to the last stanza of Marcus Wells's "Holy Spirit, Faithful Guide" (No. 210), in which we believers are depicted as "waiting still for sweet release," "wond'ring if our names were there," and "wading deep the dismal flood." Such sentiments are hardly Christian, and certainly if some might experience such doldrums they are not likely to want to sing about them.

Dr. Andrew Reed (1787-1862), a British Congregationalist, did what he could to alleviate the imbalance of hymns to the various Persons of the Trinity. Of the twenty-one hymns he wrote, only two are extant, and both of these are on the subject of the Holy Spirit. Both are in *The Hymnal*. In addition to the one under discussion, there is the beautiful "Spirit Divine, Attend Our Prayer" (No. 204), replete with its vivid images of the Spirit as light, fire, wind, and dove. Sad to state, neither of these is found in many current hymnals.

Dr. Reed, who received his D.D. degree from Yale University during a visit to the United States, was not only a pastor and writer but made a large contribution in the area of philanthropy. He was responsible for the founding of several orphanages and asylums in various parts of England.

The tune *Mercy* is one of the prime examples of hymn tunes taken from instrumental works. Others include *Hymn to Joy* (No. 21), from Beethoven's *Ninth Symphony; Canonbury* (No's. 40, 450, 484), from Schumann's *Nachtstuck*, and *Haydn* (No. 23), from Haydn's *Symphony No. 93 in D major*. Louis Moreau Gottschalk (1829-69) was a celebrated piano virtuoso during his time. Chopin heard him in his debut and said, "I predict you will become a king of pianists." P. T. Barnum offered him an enticing contract to come under his aegis—a proposition which the artist refused because of its circus implications.

His talent was quite showy, however, and dedicated largely to highly sentimental music. His own compositions were of this category, but very popular with the public. He played eighty concerts in New York City during the winter of 1855-56, at each of which he was repeatedly encored for his performances of *The Last Hope*, from which this hymn tune was taken. Dr. Edwin Pond Parker, a Congregational minister at Hartford, Connecticut, adapted the melody from the elaborate piano piece.

Chapter Eight

The Holy Scriptures

Thy statutes have been my songs in the house of my pilgrimage. —Psalm 119:54

In the logical succession of categories of praise, the worship of the triune God is closely followed by the praise of His Word. We should allot time for such recognition, for it is the Scriptures which give us our view of God, His Son, and the Christian way of life. It is here we meet the blessed Holy Spirit and learn how He can, in turn, reveal the Word to us.

Praise of the Bible is a traditional form of song, dating back to the Old Testament itself, where the Psalmist devotes many verses to the eulogy of God's Word.

The affinity of the hymnal for the Bible, of course, goes far beyond this brief section. In a very real sense the hymnal *is* the Bible, for few are the hymns which do not bear a recognizable kinship with a passage, or several passages, of Scripture. Some hymnals have included in their indexes an index of Scriptural texts and allusions. Almost every book in the Bible is included in such lists, and there are usually many more references than there are hymns.

Almighty God, Thy Word Is Cast (No. 212)   John Cawood, 1819
Belmont (C. M.)   From William Gardiner's "Sacred Melodies," 1812

The parable of the sower, recorded in Matthew 13:18-23,

is here beautifully recounted in poetic form by a little-known British curate, John Cawood (1775-1852), son of a poor farmer. This text, found in few hymnals, has a message shared by no other English hymn, to my knowledge.

The tune, *Belmont*, is one of the finest common meter melodies, and is used with many hymns. Its composer or compiler, William Gardiner (1770-1853), was one of the "characters" of hymnology. He was born and buried in Leicester, England. As a young boy he wrote considerable music, attributing it to "W. G. Leicester" (his initials plus hometown). He traveled widely during his life, making the acquaintance of as many great musicians as he could, among them Mozart, Haydn, and Beethoven. He claimed to be the first to introduce Beethoven's works in England. His occupation was to assist his father in the manufacture of stockings, but he managed to spend most of his time with his avocation: music. On one occasion he combined the two activities by weaving the opening measures of Haydn's *Austrian Hymn* (No. 416) into the "clock" of a pair of hose and presenting them to the great composer.

Gardiner was much distressed by the sacred music of his day, writing in his book *Music and Nature:* "The piety of the non-conformists has been married to unholy strains, and we have been deluged with a psalmody composed of light and impious trash."

One of his major contributions to the elevation of sacred music in his day was the publication of a six-volume work entitled *Sacred Melodies*, in which he sought to acquaint the people of England with the great masterworks. It was in this book that *Belmont* was introduced. It has been attributed to various composers, including Mozart, since Gardiner failed to label his tunes. It has been widely used, appearing three times in *The Hymnal*.

"Billy" Gardiner has been described as "a funny little figure" with a walking gait of "half-shambling and half-trotting, and he seemed in a crab-like fashion to be always following his nose. . . but in his love for music he was a prophet calling out of the darkness."

Tell Me the Old, Old Story (No. 217)   Katherine Hankey, 1866
Evangel (7. 6. 7. 6. D. with refrain)   William H. Doane, 1869

This is one of two well-known gospel songs derived from a long poem by the daughter of a London banker. Part I, consisting of fifty verses entitled "The Story Wanted," was the source of this text. Part II, called "The Story Told," gave us the sequel, "I Love to Tell the Story (No. 382).

Katherine Hankey (1834-1911), usually called Kate, was christened Arabella Catherine. Early in life she exhibited an evangelical zeal, promoting Bible study classes among working girls as well as those in her own social set. Her absorbing interest in missions was stimulated by a trip to South Africa to visit and care for an invalid brother, during which she was obliged to travel by oxcart. From that time she donated all royalties from her books and hymns to missionary work.

William Howard Doane (1832-1915) was an industrialist and inventor, the head of a large manufacturing business. He managed to find time for his absorbing avocation: that of writing music. He wrote some 2,300 songs and cantatas, among them some of our best-loved gospel song tunes. Nine of them appear in *The Hymnal*. He also edited more than forty songbooks and was very active in the ministry of Moody and Sankey. The degree of Music Doctor was conferred on him by Denison University in 1875, and in recent years Moody Bible Institute of Chicago dedicated a large pipe organ to his memory.

Chapter Nine

Invitation and Salvation

. . . the Lord Jehovah is my strength and my song; he also is become my salvation.   —Isaiah 12:2

The oft-quoted hymn definition of St. Augustine confined it to praise of God. "A hymn. . . containeth these three things," he propounded: "song, and praise, and that of God." This was adopted as canonical law at the Council of Toledo, Spain, in 633, and dominated hymn writing for several centuries.

As a general ideal this is exemplary and tends to rule out much that is unworthy in hymnody. That it is unnecessarily restrictive in practice is revealed by a look at the Pauline view that "teaching and admonishing" should be included in our singing (Col. 3:16).

Certainly the presentation of the call of Christ to repentance, dedication, and consecration should have a place in our hymnody. Here, after extolling the holiness of God, the hymn singer recognizes his own sinfulness and accepts the claims of Christ upon his life. Nowhere in *The Hymnal* can we find songs of greater consequence in the changing of lives and determining eternal destiny.

THE CALL OF CHRIST

√ **"Follow Me!" A Call So Tender (No. 223)**   A. L. Skoog, 1890
                                                Trans. by the author
√ *Ljuva röst* (8. 7. 8. 7. with refrain)   A. L. Skoog, 1890

The name of Andrew L. Skoog (1856-1934) is not an important one in the general annals of hymnology. But to the immigrant Swedish community in midwestern America in the latter nineteenth and early twentieth centuries it stood supreme. And even today, wherever the descendants of those early settlers are found, the passing of the years and the changing of musical tastes have scarcely diluted the reverence for that name. His ten hymns which are included in *The Hymnal*, a mere fragment of his large hymn output, are among the most popular in our churches.

Although trained by his father to be a tailor, A. L. Skoog was at various times—and often simultaneously—a teacher, photographer, salesman, writer, publisher, printer, Sunday school administrator, politician, poet, composer, organist, and choirmaster. Far from being a dabbler in these many areas, he actually was successful in each. To be more specific, he was an alderman on the Minneapolis City Council, the editor and publisher of a popular monthly journal in the Swedish language, superintendent of the largest Sunday school in the city, and organist-director for a tremendous church music program. At the same time countless hymns and anthems came from his pen—and on at least one occasion from a burned match on a white shirtcuff. And he had hobbies! As a painter, he showed command of line, color, and perspective. He was skilled in wood carving and furniture making, and was interested in botany, electronics, inventing, and even embroidery.

Born in Värmland, Sweden, he moved to St. Paul, Minnesota, at the age of twelve. His formal education ended with the sixth grade, but his self-imposed search for knowledge continued for a lifetime. His musical training consisted of twelve lessons on the melodeon, yet he edited seven hymnals, numerous collections of works of the masters, and even wrote a textbook on theory. Of his musical education he said: "It was obtained in the exacting school of experience. Instead of having at the start of my life put my tendencies in the sure bank of diligent study, on which I could later have drawn interest, I have factually the whole time lived on the capital. But I do not complain. Perhaps a full technical training would have drawn me away from the service where God wanted me."

That service was found in Chicago for six years and in Minneapolis for the almost fifty remaining years of his life. In this ministry his collaboration with the illustrious Pastor E. A. Skogsbergh was frequently characterized as the Swedish counterpart of the Moody and Sankey team.

Surely A. L. Skoog answered the "call so tender" and, following, led countless numbers to put their trust in the Savior whom he loved and served so fruitfully.

ANSWERING CHRIST'S CALL

I Heard the Voice of Jesus Say (No. 239)   Horatius Bonar, 1846
Vox Dilecti (C. M. D.)   John B. Dykes, 1868

The original title of this hymn was "The Voice from Galilee" and utilizes three of our Lord's sayings, as quoted in the Gospels:

"Come unto me, all ye that labor and are heavy laden and I will give you rest" (Matthew 11:28).

"Whosoever drinketh of the water that I shall give him shall never thirst" (John 4:14).

"I am the light of the world: he that followeth me shall not walk in darkness, but shall have the light of life" (John 8:12).

According to the author, however, it was based on John 1:16: "Of his fulness have all we received, and grace for grace." It is a perfectly patterned hymn, with the voice of Jesus speaking during the first half of each stanza and the reply and result in the second half.

The tune, *Vox Dilecti* ("Voice of the Beloved One"), is one of Dr. Dykes's best. (See p. 29.) He has carefully delineated the statement-response pattern of the text with minor-major sections. His adroit emphases on the important words of each stanza, particularly in the climactic last lines, is one of the prime examples of compatible text-tune wedding.

Horatius Bonar (1808-89), undoubtedly the greatest of the Scottish hymnists, was also one of the most powerful preachers of his day. He was a very devout man and a leader in the relatively rare teaching of the second coming of Christ. He kept a notebook in which he would jot down ideas for hymns during rare moments of relaxation. His involvement in many responsibilities elicited this comment: "One said of him that he was always visiting, another that he was always preaching, another that he was always writing, another that he was always praying."

PENITENCE AND CONFESSION

Just As I Am, Without One Plea (No. 250)   Charlotte Elliott, 1836
Woodworth (L. M.)   William B. Bradbury, 1849

Vivid is the childhood memory of an oft-repeated evangelistic narrative on the writing of this hymn. There seem to have been several variations on the tale, but it concerned the wayward young lady, Charlotte Elliott, who was putting off the making of a decision for Christ, and her pastor, who was pleading for her not to wait. Charlotte was just leaving for a dance, it seems, when the good minister was calling at the family home. "Don't delay," he called after her. "Come to Jesus now, *just as you are*." Amid the gaiety of the evening's merrymaking, so the story goes, Miss Elliott could not shake the memory of those last four words and, during an intermission in the dance, she slipped away by herself and gave her heart to the Lord. The hymn was written later as a result of this experience.

A rather effective story! The only difficulty is that this, like a number of "hymn stories" that have been circulated quite freely, is not true! At the time when this little drama was supposed to be taking place, Miss Charlotte Elliott (1789-1871) was a pain-wracked invalid who was most certainly not addicted to dancing.

Take away the setting, doubtless the product of some overactive imagination, and there is the essence of truth. It was in the Elliott home in Brighton, England, that Dr. Caesar Malan, the famed preacher of Geneva, led Charlotte to the Lord with the words, "You have nothing of merit to bring to God. You must come *just as you are*, a sinner, to the Lamb of God that taketh away the sin of the world." Miss Elliott always pointed to this day in 1822, when she was 33, as her spiritual birthday. The hymn was written fourteen years later when, according to her niece, Miss Elliott had spent a sleepless night, concerned about her apparent lack of usefulness. Out of this crucible of physical and mental suffering was forged by the Spirit of God this powerful expression of faith.

This hymn needs no emotional story to justify its place in the lives of several generations of Christians. D. L. Moody said it had probably touched more hearts and brought more souls to Christ than any other ever written. And almost a century has passed since he made that statement—a century during which this hymn has been the dominant invitation hymn in several countries.

It is said that among Miss Elliott's papers were found more than a thousand letters of gratitude to her for giving the world that hymn. She actually wrote 150 hymns in all, but "Just As I Am" is certainly the one which has made her to be considered the foremost of English hymn writers.

"He knows, and He alone," wrote Charlotte Elliott of her

afflictions, "what it is, day after day, hour after hour, to fight against almost overpowering weakness, languor, and exhaustion." No ballroom butterfly she, but one who knew great suffering and a greater God who "sees, guides, and guards me. His grace surrounds me, and His voice bids me to be happy and holy in His service, just where I am."

William Batchelder Bradbury (1816-68), composer of the tune *Woodworth*, was an organist, conductor, music educator, publisher, and piano manufacturer. He was largely responsible for the introduction of music teaching in the New York City public school system and was a vital link between the hymns of Lowell Mason and the later gospel songs.

Amazing Grace! How Sweet the Sound (No. 258)   John Newton (1725-1807)
Amazing Grace (C. M.)   Early American Melody

A number of people have written their own epitaphs, but few have been so frankly autobiographical as Newton when he wrote:

John Newton, Clerk
Once an infidel and libertine,
A servant of slaves in Africa;
Was by the rich mercy of our Lord and Saviour, Jesus Christ,
Preserved, restored, pardoned,
And appointed to preach the Faith
He had long laboured to destroy.
Near sixteen years at Olney in Bucks;
And twenty-seven years in this church.

But this was not the only autobiography he bequeathed. He was fond of weaving his personal testimony into his hymns. "Amazing Grace" is one of these. Another begins,
In evil long I took delight,
Unaw'd by shame or fear,

Till a new object struck my sight
And stopped my wild career.

John Newton's self-deprecation was not an extravagant glamorization of the before-and-after aspect of conversion. His is a most remarkable story. Left motherless at the age of seven, young Newton went to sea at eleven and had already set a most ignoble record before he was out of his teens. A deserter, often cruelly flogged for his offences, a slave trader, a man so vile that his fellow sailors frequently protested his language and actions. Then at the age of twenty-three came a cataclysmic conversion which led ultimately to leadership in the evangelical wing of the Church of England and immortality in the annals of hymnology.

In collaboration with his friend William Cowper, Newton published the *Olney Hymns*, the first great hymnal of the Anglican Church. Of the 349 hymns, 283 were written by Newton, the remaining 66 being by Cowper. Only a few of these remain in general use, but they are among the best in current hymnals, including "Safely Through Another Week" (No. 25), "How Sweet the Name of Jesus Sounds" (No. 385), and "Glorious Things of Thee Are Spoken" (No. 416).

Newton was pastor at Olney, near Cambridge, for sixteen years. Moving to St. Mary Woolnoth, in London, he was active until his death. When he was past eighty and had lost his eyesight, his friends urged him to give up preaching. His reply: "What, shall the old African blasphemer stop while he can speak!"

"Amazing Grace" originally consisted of six stanzas bearing the title "Faith's Review and Expectation" and was based on 1 Chronicles 17:16, 17: "And David the king came and sat before the Lord, and said, Who am I, O Lord God, and what is mine house, that thou hast brought me hitherto? And yet this was a small thing in thine eyes, O God; for thou hast also spoken of thy servant's house for a great while to come, and hast regarded me according to the estate of a man of high degree, O Lord God." The stanza beginning "When we've been there ten thousand years" was not written by Newton, being added more than a century later.

The tune is of unknown origin but is presumably from the Southeastern states, appearing first in a tune book titled *Virginia Harmony* in 1831.

DEDICATION AND CONSECRATION

Jesus, Lover of My Soul (No. 271)   Charles Wesley. 1740
Martyn (7. 7. 7. 7. D.)   Simeon B. Marsh, 1834

Superlative statements literally cluster about this hymn. "The finest hymn in the English language" (Telford); "It shares with the 23rd Psalm first place in the hearts of countless thousands" (Sutherland); "Scarcely any hymn . . . can dispute supremacy with this" (Duffield); "One which the entire church, with absolute unanimity, assigns to the first place" (Breed); "The best-loved hymn in the language; the favorite of learned and illiterate, high and humble" (Benson); "I would rather have written that hymn of Charles Wesley's than to have the fame of all the kings that ever sat on the earth" (Beecher).

Charles Wesley (1707-88) wrote some 6,500 hymns. He wrote them daily—during personal devotions, while dining, even while on horseback. His friends were accustomed to hearing the clop of hoofs outside their doors and the urgent voice of Charles Wesley calling, "Pen and ink! Pen and ink!" Another hymn was waiting to be born. His diary records a revealing item as he tells of being thrown from his horse one day: "My companions thought I had broken my neck; but my leg only was bruised, my hand sprained, and my head stunned, *which spoiled my making hymns until next day.*"

The unreliability of many hymn stories is attested by the fact that there are three generally accepted tales concerning this song, no two of which could be true. Take your choice. (1) A bird, escaping from a hawk, flew through a window into a room in which Charles was sitting. (2) Fleeing from a mob, Wesley hid in a hedge for refuge, writing the hymn while there. (3) During a storm at sea, a bedrenched seabird flew through an open porthole into Wesley's cabin.

Whatever the story of its origin, there are many verified stories of the potent and far-reaching ministry of these lines. Kings and peasants have passed out of this life with its words on their lips. Translated into almost every known tongue, it has been the means of blessing to multiplied thousands for two centuries.

If greatness has a kinship with simplicity, this hymn is a model. Of the 188 words used, 157 are of one syllable, leaving only 31 polysyllabic words! The third stanza—possibly the greatest—uses only three words of more than one syllable.

Many tunes have been used with this hymn, the best-known in America being *Martyn*, written by Simeon Butler Marsh (1798-1875) in Sherburne, New York.

Chapter Ten

The Life in Christ

. . . teaching and admonishing one another in psalms and hymns and spiritual songs.   —Colossians 3:16

We come now to the largest single section of *The Hymnal*, dealing with several aspects of Christian life and activity. And here, incidentally, we find the greatest number of so-called "gospel songs." The term is something of a misnomer since, far from having a corner on the gospel, they contain less of the gospel message than the general body of hymns. The word "gospel," derived from two Anglo-Saxon words meaning good news, is generally conceded to refer to the revelation of the goodness of God in the person of the Lord Jesus Christ and deals with His incarnation, atoning death, resurrection, ascension, His intercessory position at the right hand of God, and His second coming. This is the gospel, and its message is largely covered in section five of *The Hymnal*, "Jesus Christ the Lord," and our relationship to the gospel message is dealt with in section eight, "Invitation and Salvation." The gospel song, as it is generally known today, was a development of the latter half of the nineteenth century—a label attached to the popularized songs of the Moody-Sankey revivals and to all subsequent songs of the same type. They are characterized by simple, popular tunes which usually include a refrain, with texts of a repetitive and sentimental nature. They dip into a wide range of subject matter, majoring on the alpha and the omega of the Christian life, i.e., salvation and heaven. Many of the most useful gospel songs, however, are those which deal with the day-to-day life of the Christian. Being primarily subjective and experiential, they are well adapted to this area. Even so, this subject matter is amply covered by the standard hymns, for although this section contains more gospel songs than any other—about 45—there are still a great many more—some 83— which would be classified as true hymns.

Whatever the appellation, the songs in this category are among the most used in the entire volume, dealing with a wide range of subjects pertinent to Christian living.

PRAYER AND INTERCESSION

Lord, I Hear of Showers of Blessing (No. 292) Elizabeth Codner, 1860
Even Me (8. 7. 8. 7. with refrain)   William B. Bradbury, 1862

Mrs. Elizabeth Codner (1824-1919), wife of a London minister, had been reading in the Old Testament. A verse in Ezekiel impressed her. It was chapter 34, verse 26, which reads: "And I will make them and the places round about my hill a blessing; and I will cause the shower to come down in his season; there shall be showers of blessing." She thought of other similar passages, such as Psalm 72, which speaks of the rain coming down upon the mown grass and the "showers that water the earth" and their relationship to the dry and arid regions of Palestine. How important were their wells and cisterns! And when they were dry or filled up by their enemies, how the children of Israel needed those "showers of blessing"!

Mrs. Codner's musings were interrupted by a group of young people who came to tell her of their exciting visit to Ireland. A great spiritual awakening was sweeping over certain cities and counties of the Emerald Isle, and they had been thrilled by its impact upon the people. While they were recounting their experiences, the devout lady was praying that these young people would not be content to have been mere spectators of the Holy Spirit's working. Impulsively, with the words of Ezekiel in mind, she said, "While the Lord is pouring out such showers of blessing, pray that some drops will fall on each of you."

The following Sunday morning, while Mrs. Codner remained home from her husband's church due to illness, she wrote the stanzas as we have them. Leaflets containing the poem came to the attention of American composer William B. Bradbury, who set them to music.

ASPIRATION

O for a Faith That Will Not Shrink   William H. Bathurst, 1831
  (No. 301)
Evan (C. M.)   William H. Havergal, 1846

Among the little "two-liners" in *The Hymnal* that may often be overlooked is this challenging delineation of an overcoming faith. Actually, the text is made up of quatrains, but the musical phrases reduce it to two lines per stanza.

As in most of our hymns, there have been stanzas omitted. Sometimes this contemporary practice robs us of some rich lyrics, but in more cases one finds that the awkward or unnecessary stanzas have been eliminated. Such is the case here. Note this omitted stanza:

> *That bears unmoved the world's dread frown,*
>   *Nor heeds its scornful smile;*
> *That sin's wild ocean cannot drown,*
>   *Nor its soft arts beguile.*

Just as the modern preacher finds he can say in twenty-five minutes what his ministerial forebears would have expanded into an hour's discourse, so our present-day editors have found that the multiplicity of stanzas often adds little but verbiage to the presentation of truth.

This does in no way condone the thoughtless mutilation of hymns which is the common practice of many ministers and song leaders. The casual abbreviation by merely calling out, "First, second, and last stanzas, please" often leads to abortive and confusing expressions.

One thinks of a hymn such as "A Mighty Fortress Is Our God," in which the omission of the third stanza utterly destroys the continuity. The last stanza begins with the phrase

> *That word above all earthly pow'rs,*
> *No thanks to them, abideth.*

What word? The last phrase of the preceding stanza explains it:

> *One little word shall fell him.*

Omit that stanza, and you have garbled thoughts. Worse yet is the instance when the leader suggested that we "stand and sing one stanza of 'A Mighty Fortress.'" A quick glance down the lines of that first stanza reveals that it is in praise of the Devil! It speaks of the effectiveness of the craft and power of "our ancient foe" and closes with the discouraging phrase "On earth is not his equal." It takes the next stanza to point out the only way to defeat him.

No stanzas should be omitted from the present version of Dr. Bathurst's stalwart hymn. It is from his collection called *Psalms and Hymns for Public and Private Use* and is an exposition of Luke 17:5, originally titled "The Power of Faith." Its first three stanzas describe true victorious faith, and the last is a personal affirmation of this faith.

William Hiley Bathurst (1796-1877) was an Oxford graduate—one of a considerable group of early-nineteenth-century Anglican rectors who made contributions to the body of hymnody. He wrote more than 200 hymns and 100 Psalm versions.

William Henry Havergal (1793-1870), the composer of the tune *Evan*, was also prominent in the Church of England and wrote many hymns and other musical works. The family name received even more luster through the genius of his famous daughter, Frances Ridley Havergal, one of the greatest of women hymn writers.

LOYALTY AND COURAGE

Stand Fast for Christ Thy Savior (No. 311)   Walter J. Mathams, 1913
Alford (7. 6. 8. 6. D.)   John B. Dykes, 1875

Here is a typical "teaching and admonishing" type of song. It is neither directed to God nor to the unconverted man but to all of Christ's followers in a spiritual challenge.

The scriptural inspiration for the hymn doubtless came from the exhortation in 1 Corinthians 16:13 to "stand fast in the faith." The strong figures of speech used describe the lighthouse with its granite foundation and the stouthearted soldier who stands fearlessly until the battle is over. Finally, the supreme example is given of the Savior who "once stood fast for thee."

This is one of our finest early-twentieth-century hymns, but it has found its way into few American hymnals. It was written by the British Baptist, Walter John Mathams (1853-1932). Mathams' story seems to parallel that of John Newton, famed English hymnwriter who lived nearly two centuries earlier. He went to sea as a youth, was shipwrecked, and later forced into the Brazilian army in its war with Paraguay. Converted during a trip through Palestine, he began to study for the ministry, later filling a number of pastorates in England. He served as a chaplain in Egypt, then became a member of the established Church of Scotland. He wrote a number of books and many hymns, all with a strong emphasis upon youth.

Dr. John B. Dykes's tune *Alford* was named after Dean Henry Alford, author of "Ten Thousand Times Ten Thousand," for which hymn the tune was written.

FAITH AND ASSURANCE

Blessed Assurance, Jesus Is Mine!   Fanny J. Crosby (1820-1915)
   (No. 322)
Assurance (9. 10. 9. 9. with refrain)   Mrs. Joseph F. Knapp, 1873

Fanny Crosby (Frances Jane Crosby Van Alstyne) was America's best-known woman hymnwriter and one of the dominant writers of the entire gospel song movement. Some 8,000 songs flowed from her facile pen—a fact all the more remarkable when one considers her lifelong blindness and that she wrote her first hymn at age forty-one.

Fanny Crosby was blinded at the age of six weeks due to improper treatment by a country doctor. Far from being depressed by her affliction, she felt it to be a blessing. At the age of eight she expressed her philosophy in this bit of cheerful verse:

> *O what a happy soul am I!*
> *Although I cannot see,*
> *I am resolved that in this world*
> *Contented I will be.*
>
> *How many blessings I enjoy,*
> *That other people don't;*
> *To weep and sigh because I'm blind,*
> *I cannot, and I won't!*

The strong scriptural tone of her songs attests her knowledge of the Bible. As a child she committed to memory long passages, including the first four books of the Old Testament and the four Gospels.

Miss Crosby married Alexander Van Alstyne, a blind musician, in 1858, and they spent forty-four years together, helping each other.

Fanny Crosby wrote her songs with incredible speed, often completing them while conversation went on about her. One day Philip Phillips, the "singing pilgrim," came to her with forty subjects for hymns. He returned several days later and found that she had completed them all and could quote them from memory.

Thirteen of her songs are included in *The Hymnal*, none better loved than "Blessed Assurance." Of it she said, "My friend, Mrs. Knapp, composed a melody, and played it over to me two or three times on the piano. She then asked me what it said, and I immediately replied, 'Blessed Assurance.' " A few minutes later she had completed the poem just as it stands today.

Mrs. Joseph F. Knapp (1839-1908) was born Phoebe Palmer, daughter of a noted Methodist evangelist. At the age of sixteen she married Joseph Fairchild Knapp, a wealthy Christian businessman, founder of the Metropolitan Life Insurance Company. She published over 500 of her own songs and compositions, including the solo "Open the Gates of the Temple," in which she again collaborated with Fanny Crosby.

Day by Day Thy Mercies, Lord,   Lina Sandell, 1865
   Attend Me (No. 325)   Trans. by Ernest Edwin Ryden, 1928
Blott en dag (10. 9. 10. 9. D.)   Oscar Ahnfelt (1813-82)

"The Swedish Fanny Crosby" is one of the appellations used to describe the beloved poetess, Lina Sandell (1832-1903). And there are interesting parallels to be found between the two feminine lyricists. They were contemporary, although Fanny Crosby was born earlier and died later than her Swedish counterpart. There is something similar too in the fact that they were both known by abbreviated versions of their maiden names, even after they were married. The one, born Frances Jane Crosby, was always "Fanny Crosby" even after she became the wife of Alexander Van Alstyne. The other was born Caroline Wilhelmina Sandell but was known as "Lina Sandell" even after she married Oscar Berg.

Like Fanny Crosby, Lina Sandell began to write at an early age and wrote prolifically. Her first book of poems came off the press when she was just thirteen. More than 30 songs came from this first collection, and over 150 of her songs have found a degree of successful usage.

Miss Sandell did not suffer the handicap of blindness which her American likeness endured, but she was frail as a child and underwent a great deal of suffering and tragedy. While on a trip with her father through the Göta Kanal, he fell overboard and drowned. In her great sorrow she penned the lovely *Kommer du ej snart*—"Hide Not Thy Face, O My Savior" (No. 507)—a song that was to be immortalized, together with its plaintive Finnish melody, in Dr. F. M. Christiansen's "Lost in the Night."

Ten of Lina Sandell's lovely hymns in fine translations have been included in *The Hymnal*. Our subject hymn has had an earlier translation by A. L. Skoog which is much more popular and, in the opinion of experts in the language such as Dr. Obed Johnson, more accurate. We are indebted to Dr. Johnson for his translation of the following interesting narrative taken from the Swedish book of hymnist biographies, *Våra Psalm- och Sångdiktare*, by Oscar Lövgren.

For a number of years Lina Sandell published a "Bible Calendar" of inspirational articles. Some of her best songs first appeared in this form, including "*Blott en dag,*" which was found in the first edition. The following allegory gave rise to the song:

The old wall clock, which for more than fifty years had been faithfully recording the passage of time, had suddenly stopped. The clock dial decided to make a thorough investigation to determine the cause of this tragedy. During the course of this investigation it became perfectly clear that the pendulum was to blame. It had simply gone on strike. Why? By exact calculation it had figured out that during the next twenty-four hours it was expected to swing back and forth no less than 86,400 times and, as it continued to multiply this figure by hours, days, months and years, it lost courage completely and simply stopped working. The clock dial seemed amazed at the pendulum's action and at its type of reasoning. It admitted that the pendulum had much work to do, but then, who didn't? It also affirmed that it was not the work itself, but rather the thought of the work, which seemed to paralyze the pendulum. It also expressed the wish that the pendulum would kindly resume its work temporarily and swing back and forth in customary fashion just six times. The pendulum agreed and, after faithful performance of duty, frankly admitted that it did not feel the least bit weary, but the reason for that, it insisted, was that its back and forth movements were so few. "It's not the thought of the six or the sixty times that disturbs me," the pendulum said, "but rather the thought of more than six million times."

"Well and good," replied the clock dial, "but please bear this in mind: while in just a single moment you can envisage the millions of movements you are required to make in a lifetime, do not forget that only one back and forth swing at a time will be required of you, and for that moment ample time will be provided." After due consideration the pendulum admitted that it had acted very foolishly in going on a strike and promptly resumed its useful work.

Thus was born "*Blott en dag, ett ögonblick i sän-der*"—"Just a day, just a moment, marks the passage of time."

COMFORT AND PEACE

When Peace, Like a River, Attendeth   Horatio G. Spafford, 1876
  My Way (No. 365)
It is well with my soul (Irregular with refrain)   P. P. Bliss, 1876

One of the most dramatic and touching of hymn stories is the one associated with this gospel song. "Authentic" accounts differ on certain points, but the general facts are agreed upon.

Horatio G. Spafford (1828-88), a prominent Chicago lawyer, planned a European trip for his family, primarily for his wife's health. They secured passage on the S. S. *Ville du Havre* in November of 1873. Sudden business demands made it necessary for Mr. Spafford to remain in Chicago for a while, and he sent his wife and four children on ahead, expecting to join them later. Their ship was struck in mid-ocean by an English sailing vessel and sank in twelve minutes. The four daughters perished, but Mrs. Spafford was rescued by a sailor and brought to Cardiff, Wales, where she cabled her husband the cryptic message "Saved alone."

The distraught husband left immediately to meet his wife. Evangelist D. L. Moody, a personal friend of the family, left meetings in Edinburgh to comfort the bereaved parents. He found that "the God of all comfort" had already met them, and Mr. Spafford was able to say, "It is well; the will of God be done."

Ira D. Sankey said that it was three years later, while

he was entertained in the Spafford home, that the hymn was written. Bertha Spafford Vester, a daughter, said that it was written on the high seas near the scene of the tragedy while Spafford was on his way to meet his wife. Whatever the details, we know this to be one of the most inspiring songs to come out of the gospel song movement.

Philip Paul Bliss (1838-76), one of the most prolific and effective of the gospel song composers, provided the musical setting, sometimes titled *Ville du Havre* after the ill-fated ship. It is worthy of note that this hymn, born in tragedy, was one of the last songs to be written and sung by Mr. Bliss before his sudden death in a train accident on December 29, 1876. Bliss had gone back into the flaming wooden coach to rescue his wife. Failing in the attempt, the thirty-eight-year-old singer died by her side. His very last song, found in a trunk which had reached Chicago safely, began: "I know not what awaits me; God kindly veils my eyes. . ."

✓ **I Sing with Joy and Gladness (No. 355)** Nils Frykman, 1881
            Trans. by E. Gustav Johnson, 1946
✓ *Nu är jag nöjd* (13. 13. 13. 8.)   Nils Frykman, 1881

This hymn is a good example of the many hymns produced by one of the very best Swedish-American hymnists, Nils Frykman (1842-1911), called by Swedish hymnographer Oscar Lövgren "the singer of Christian gladness and good cheer."

It was on October 20, 1842, that the pastor of the little parish church of Sunne, in Värmland, Sweden, made a routine entry in his register: "Born this day to L. Larson and his wife Kerstin, a son." So another Larson—Nils, by name —takes his first lungful of Swedish air. Certainly nothing unusual about that!

Yet here was born one who was to become a power in the

rising free church movement in Sweden, one who was to be chosen to collaborate with two other church leaders in setting down the tenets of the Swedish Evangelical Mission Covenant Church in America, one whose delightful lyrics and tunes would bring spiritual refreshment to people a century removed and thousands of miles as well. We do not remember him as Nils Larson, however, but as Nils Frykman. In 1866, when he registered as a student in a teachers college in Karlstad, he decided to change his surname to Frykman, after his native Fryksdalen.

If he were to be asked how he, born into poverty and left fatherless as a young lad, could have left his mark upon thousands of people on two continents, he could find no better words than those of his own hymn, "Our Mighty God Works Mighty Wonders" (No. 66).

Frykman became a school teacher, but he was so caught up in the religious awakening that was sweeping through his home province that all of his free time was spent attending the revival services which were held almost day and night in various homes throughout the area. Soon he was leading services of his own, preaching and singing.

Although Nils Frykman wrote more than 300 songs in his time, he was thirty-three years of age before he wrote his first one. It was actually a revision of an old hymn which he felt was poorly written. From that time on he wrote freely and frequently, but never on order. Only when the inspiration was upon him could he set down his thoughts in verse, and this came at various odd moments. He was preaching at one time when a visitor from a long distance away walked into the service. Seeing the large, enthusiastic group crowded into the small home, the stranger's look of amazement seemed to say, "What in the world is happening here?" Frykman "felt a song coming on," so he hastily concluded his sermon, allowed another man to take over the preaching duties, and sat down at a little table behind the speaker. There he wrote the song previously referred to—"Our Mighty God Works Mighty Wonders." He kept paper and pencil near him wherever he went so that he could jot down his songs as they came.

And they came quite regularly—and all with the theme of joyful Christian optimism: "The Highest Joy That Can Be Known" (No. 220), "List to the Gospel Resounding" (No. 231), "I Have a Friend Who Loveth Me" (No. 370), "When My Lord Is Dear to Me" (No. 377), "How Wonderful It Is" (No. 433), "I Have a Future All Sublime" (No. 512).

There came a time when the state church, not at all in sympathy with the pietistic movement, decided to close in on Frykman and his friends. They could not interfere with his preaching in the homes, but they attacked him in his public school teaching, where religion was one of the subjects offered. Bishops visited the school in 1880 to investigate, with the result that he and two of his fellow teachers were subjected to a formal trial to answer accusations regarding the orthodoxy of their theology. They were allowed to go back to their teaching temporarily but under sharp warnings to "mend their ways." This was the occasion for the writing of "I Sing with Joy and Gladness" (No. 355), expressing both his theology and his dauntless spirit.

This was the spirit which later led him to leave the teaching field altogether and to devote himself entirely to preaching, then to accept a call from across the waters to become pastor of the Swedish Mission Tabernacle Church in Chicago, and finally to leave the big city for five tiny churches in Kandiyohi County of Minnesota, where for eight years he traveled back and forth among the parishes, laboring under the most primitive and trying conditions. It was there that he penned the lines "My Savior's love so full and free/ Doth light the weary way for me;/ It fills with joy each passing day/ And drives my sorrows all away."

JOY

Come, We That Love the Lord (No. 368)   Isaac Watts, 1707
Marching to Zion   Robert Lowry (1826-99)
(6. 6. 8. 8. 6. 6. with refrain)

Isaac Watts (1674-1748) was peculiarly fitted for his role of "father of the English hymn." Parental influence, native ability, and environmental conditions all united to produce one who was to change the singing habits of all English-speaking peoples.

His father was a courageous Dissenter, whose several imprisonments would not deter him from seeking to change the unhealthy spiritual conditions of the time. When Isaac, as yet only a teen-ager, criticized the inordinately low standards of singing in the church, it was his father who both rebuked and challenged him with the words, "Give us something better, young man." Before the day was over, the boy had written his first hymn:

> *Behold the glories of the Lamb*
> *Amid his Father's throne,*
> *Prepare new honors for His name,*
> *And songs before unknown.*

It was sung that very evening in the chapel, and for the next two years Isaac Watts supplied a new hymn each Sunday for use in the church. It was the breakthrough that ultimately loosed the stranglehold of the Metrical Psalm upon the church singing of Britain.

Watts's talent manifested itself at an early age. He was taught Latin at the age of four, Greek at eight or nine, French at eleven, and Hebrew at thirteen. He had a remarkable—and oft annoying—gift of speaking in rhyme. Once, during family prayers, little Isaac spied a mouse running up the bell rope of the clock and laughed out loud.

When an explanation for this irreverence was demanded of him, the small boy extemporized:

> *A mouse, for want of better stairs,*
> *Ran up a rope to say his prayers.*

His penchant for poetry was not always appreciated by his family, but when his father decided to "spank the rhymes out of him" the tearful face looked up and out came the words:

> *Dear father, do some pity take,*
> *And I will no more verses make.*

Watts became a Congregationalist minister, but ill health made it difficult for him to fulfil his duties. His frail frame would probably have thwarted his destiny were it not for a visit to the country estate of Sir Thomas and Lady Abney, who were very fond of the young cleric. It was to have been a week's stay. It stretched into thirty-six years, or until his death! It was during this time that Isaac Watts, his needs cared for by his remarkable benefactors, accomplished the bulk of his life's work: some sixty volumes of books on such diversified subjects as logic, astronomy and geography, and about 600 hymns.

He is represented some thirteen times in *The Hymnal.* Indeed, a hymnal would scarce be worthy of the name without "O God, Our Help in Ages Past" (No. 65), "Joy to the World!" (No. 119), "Alas! and Did My Savior Bleed" (No. 142), "When I Survey the Wondrous Cross" (No. 155), "Am I a Soldier of the Cross?" (No. 265) and "Jesus Shall Reign" (No. 460).

The general reaction to "Watts's whims" during his time was violent, and one London pastor who had joined the crusade for the use of hymns always used psalms during the main body of the service, reserving the hymn of the morning until the close so that those who had opposing convictions could leave. A commentator of the period recounted the angry exit of more than half of a congregation "before the vile thing came on," with many others visibly abstaining while the few joined in the singing. Tempers frequently flared, and some churches were split in the heat of the decidedly unharmonious musical controversy.

"Come, We That Love the Lord" contains some well-directed barbs for those who were prone to sit silent during the singing of anything but a version of the Psalms of David. A subtle suggestion occurs even in the first line: "Come, *we that love the Lord,*/ And let our joys be known./ Join in a song *with sweet accord.*" The second stanza begins in a much more direct way: "Let those refuse to sing/ Who never knew our God;/ But children of the heavenly King/ May speak their joys abroad."

Many minor textual changes have been made in this hymn during the years—more than a hundred, according to Julian—and stanzas 1, 3, 8, and 10 are the only ones remaining of the original ten-stanza hymn. Robert Lowry, composer of the tune, added the refrain, making of it a typical gospel song.

The original title of the hymn was "Heavenly Joy on Earth," later changed by John Wesley to "Heaven Begun on Earth."

LOVE AND COMMUNION

O Love That Wilt Not Let Me Go (No. 390) George Matheson, 1882
St. Margaret (8. 8. 8. 8. 6.)   Albert L. Peace, 1885

Dr. George Matheson (1842-1906) called this, his most famous hymn, "the fruit of pain." The specific causal pain can but be a matter of conjecture. He said, "Something had happened to me, which was known only to myself, and which caused me the most severe mental suffering. My hymn was composed in the manse of Innellan. . . . I was at that time alone. It was the day of my sister's marriage, and the rest of the family were staying overnight in Glasgow." Some have suggested that his sister's imminent marriage may have evoked painful memories of a time when—twenty years before—he had been engaged to be married. He was a student at the University of Glasgow at the time, and there was the promise of a brilliant career before him. Then tragedy struck! The eye condition which had plagued him since early boyhood culminated in blindness. It was at this time that his fiancee decided she could not share life with a blind man. It is not illogical to suppose that the hymn about the unwavering love of God might have been the outgrowth of that unhappy incident—not an impulsive outburst but one tempered by twenty years of experiencing that divine love.

Whatever the suffering was that blossomed into this splendid hymn, it assumed the character of remarkable inspiration. "It was the quickest bit of work I ever did in my life," said Dr. Matheson. "I had the impression rather of having it dictated to me by some inward voice than of working it out by myself. I am quite sure that the whole work was completed in five minutes, and equally sure that it never received at my hands any retouching or correction. The Hymnal Committee of the Church of Scotland desired the change of one word. I had written originally 'I climbed the rainbow in the rain.' They objected to the word 'climb' and I put in 'trace.' "

Dr. Matheson was one of Scotland's greatest pulpit voices, and his devotional and theological writings are still frequently read and quoted. Among his grateful listeners was none other than Queen Victoria, who expressed amazement at his prodigious memorization of the Scriptures and hymns.

The *St. Margaret* tune is scarcely less amazing in its inspirational origin than Matheson's text. Of it Dr. Albert Lister Peace (1844-1912) said, "It was composed . . . during the time the music of *The Scottish Hymnal,* of which I was the musical editor, was in preparation. I wrote it at Brodick Manse, where I was on a visit to my old friend, Mr. M'Lean. There was no tune of that particular metre available at that time, so I was requested by the Hymnal Committee to write one especially for Dr. Matheson's hymn. After reading it over carefully, I wrote the music straight off, and may say that the ink of the first note was hardly dry when I had finished the tune."

Dr. Peace had been a musical prodigy, with evidence of the sense of absolute pitch at the age of four. He became parish organist at Holmfirth, England, when only nine, progressing eventually to the position at Glasgow Cathedral and nation-wide fame. One preacher in a church served by Dr. Peace feared to announce the hymn "Peace, Perfect Peace" lest it be considered a personal compliment to the organist!

INNER LIFE

I Need Thee Every Hour (No. 395) Annie S. Hawks, 1872
Refrain added by Robert Lowry
Need (6. 4. 6. 4. with refrain) Robert Lowry, 1872

Annie Sherwood (Mrs. Charles H.) Hawks (1835-1918) was a housewife and a faithful member of the Hanson Place Baptist Church of Brooklyn, New York, for many years. Dr. Robert Lowry (1826-99), well-known writer of gospel songs, was her pastor. She was in her middle thirties when Dr. Lowry—who wrote no songs until he was forty—discovered her talent and encouraged her to write hymns.

She wrote more than four hundred—mainly Sunday school songs—of which this is the only survivor.

Based on the text "Without me ye can do nothing" (John 15:5), it was first sung at a meeting of the National Baptist Sunday School Association held in Cincinnati. Of it Mrs. Hawks said, "Whenever my attention is called to it I am conscious of great satisfaction in the thought that I was permitted to write the hymn . . . and that it was wafted out to the world on the wings of love and joy, rather than under the stress of a great personal sorrow, with which it has so often been associated in the minds of those who sing it.

"I remember well the morning . . . when in the midst of the daily cares of my home . . . I was so filled with the sense of nearness to the Master that, wondering how one could live without Him either in joy or pain, these words, 'I need Thee every hour,' were ushered into my mind, the thought at once taking full possession of me . . . .

"For myself the hymn was prophetic rather than expressive of my own experience at the time it was written, and I do not understand why it so touched the great throbbing heart of humanity. It was not until long years after, when the shadow fell over my way—the shadow of a great loss—that I understood something of the comforting in the words I had been permitted to write and give out to others in my hours of sweet security and peace."

Chapter Eleven

The Church
and the Sacraments

And when they had sung an hymn, they went out into the mount of Olives.   —Matthew 26:30

Music has ever been associated with the church—visible and invisible—and its sacraments. The Body of Christ has delighted to give corporate expression to the praises and petitions of its fellowship. Its sacraments and sacred occasions have customarily been accompanied by music. The only record of singing during the ministry of Christ on earth is the Matthew account quoted above (echoed verbatim by Mark in 14:26) of the first Lord's Supper. The "hymn" was doubtless a portion of the "Hallel" from Psalm 115 to 118.

THE CHURCH

Christ Is Made the Sure	Anonymous (Latin, 7th century)
Foundation (No. 413)	Trans. by John M. Neale, 1851
Regent Square (8. 7. 8. 7. 8. 7.)	Henry Smart, 1867

In church music circles one hears rather frequent reference to Gregorian music. The allusion is to the form of liturgical music developed under Gregory the Great in the sixth century. We cannot here discuss at any length this form of chant, which has been retained in some branches of the church for 1400 years. Suffice it to say that this is church music in what is possibly its purest state and deserves more than passing consideration in our quest for worthy worship media.

What is not always noted is that Gregory, in making a lasting contribution to the field of liturgical choral music, rendered a disservice to an even more important area in church music—congregational singing. From that time until the Reformation—about a thousand years—the common people were reduced to silent worshipers, the active liturgy being sung by trained clerics.

The seventh century absorbed the full force of the change, producing no hymnwriter of note. A very few Latin hymns made their appearance anonymously, some of them destined for survival. A fine example is this hymn, translated by John Mason Neale (1818-66), a most remarkable Englishman who did more than any other person to make available the rich Greek and Latin hymns.

Dr. Neale was one of the greatest and most devout of scholars—and one of the least recognized. A brilliant man with a working knowledge of twenty languages, he lived on less than $150 a year. He lived and worked among the poor, founding an orphanage, one of the first nursing schools in England, and a home for the reclamation of fallen women. He was looked down upon by his Church of England, which apparently approved of the humble epitaph he asked to have inscribed on his coffin: "J. M. Neale, poor and unworthy priest resting under the sign of the Cross."

Henry Thomas Smart (1813-79) was the son of a violinist and piano manufacturer and nephew of Sir George Thomas Smart, one of England's greatest conductors and organists. He studied for the legal profession, which he followed for just four years, then turned to music. Largely self-taught, he became one of the best organists in the British Isles and an outstanding composer of the Romantic school of church music. One writer opined that his work determined the harmonic structure of the English hymn-tune fully as much as Bach did that of the German chorale.

Henry Smart was totally blind for his last fifteen years, but a marvelously retentive memory enabled him to continue all of his musical work. Some of his finest music was composed during this time, including *Regent Square*, which appears three times in *The Hymnal*.

CHRISTIAN FELLOWSHIP

Blest Be the Tie That Binds (No. 420)   John Fawcett, 1782
Dennis (S. M.)   Arr. from Hans G. Naegeli by Lowell Mason, 1845

We have been known to speak somewhat deprecatingly of the "hymn story" on occasion. It is true that some of the most fascinating narratives have proven to be spurious and misleading. And it is also true that some really great hymns have been neglected by our more superficial hymnologists because there are no glamorous legends with which to identify them. A great hymn, like all great works, should stand on its own merits and need not have been the product of some cataclysmic event in the life of its author.

Having said this, we must hastily add that a remarkably large number of hymns have been the product of special experiences. That a knowledge of this background information can enrich our understanding and appreciation of the hymn is without question. We have included a number of such incidents in this volume.

One of the classic examples of the experiential hymn is this greatest of Christian fellowship hymns. The story of a small-town pastor, John Fawcett (1740-1817), who accepted a call to a large London church only to later retract and remain with his flock, is one of the most interesting in all hymnody. We quote the account as given by Joseph Belcher not long after the event took place:

He preached his farewell sermon to his church in Yorkshire and loaded six or seven wagons with his furniture, books, etc., to be carried to his new residence. All this time the members of his poor church were almost brokenhearted; fervently did they pray that even now he might not leave them; and as the time for his departure arrived, men, women, and children clung around him and his family in perfect agony of soul. The last wagon was being loaded, when the good man and his wife sat down on the packing cases to weep. Looking into his tearful face, while tears . . . fell down her own cheeks, his devoted wife said, "O John, John, I cannot bear this! I know not how to go!" "Nor I, either," said the good man: "Nor will we go; unload the wagons, and put everything in the place where it was before." The people cried for joy. A letter was sent to London to tell them that his coming to them was impossible; and the good man buckled on his armor for renewed labors, on a salary of less than $200 a year.

The hymn "Blest Be the Tie That Binds" is a perpetual memorial to the interesting event.

"Lord, Dismiss Us with Thy Blessing" (No. 53) and "How Precious Is the Book Divine" (No. 213) are other hymns by Fawcett included in *The Hymnal*.

The composer of the tune *Dennis* is Hans G. Naegeli (1768-1836). Born at Wetezikon, near Zurich, he was a music publisher there and president of the Swiss Association for the Cultivation of Music. He published much of Beethoven's music, including three of his piano sonatas. It is rumored that he actually suceeded in interpolating four measures into one of the sonata movements. Pardoned for his crime, he continued on most affectionate terms with the great master.

The tune *Dennis* was purchased by Lowell Mason (1792-

1872), known as the father of American church music, while in Europe in 1837 and brought back with him to enrich his hymn books. Largely self-educated, Mason owed his unquestioned success to perseverance, energy, and enthusiasm. A leader in the teaching of public school music, his teachers' conventions drew musicians from all over the nation.

BAPTISM

See Israel's Gentle Shepherd Stand (No. 423) Philip Doddridge, 1755
Serenity (C. M.)   William V. Wallace, 1856

Based on a portion of Mark 10:14, "Suffer the little children to come unto me, and forbid them not: for of such is the kingdom of God," this hymn originally bore the title "Christ's condescending Regard for little Children." It was written to follow a sermon, as were most of the more than 400 hymns of Philip Doddridge (1702-51). Doddridge, the youngest of the twenty children of a London merchant, was orphaned at an early age. The Duchess of Bedford offered to educate him for ministry in the Church of England, but he declined, becoming instead an outstanding minister and seminary professor in the nonconformist group. He was born but a few years before Wesley and died almost forty years before the great Methodist writer who, with Watts, was his inspiration.

Other Doddridge hymns in current use are: "Awake, My Soul, Stretch Every Nerve" (No. 304), "O Happy Day, That Fixed My Choice" (No. 371), "Great God, We Sing That Mighty Hand" (No. 548), and "Our Helper, God, We Bless Thy Name" (No. 549).

The fluent tune S*erenity*, also used with Whittier's "Immortal Love, Forever Full" (No. 132), is an arrangement from "Ye Winds That Waft," composed by William Vincent Wallace (1814-65), a most colorful Irish violinist and composer. He traveled during most of his life, giving concerts and writing prolifically in almost every form from operas to hymn tunes.

THE LORD'S SUPPER

According to Thy Gracious Word (No. 427) James Montgomery, 1825
Martyrdom (C. M.)   Hugh Wilson (1764-1824)

This hymn is a reply to our Lord's injunction, ". . . this do in remembrance of me," and is a moving part of many communion services. Its author, James Montgomery (1771-1854), was born in Scotland of Moravian missionary parents. Intending to prepare for the ministry, his scholastic record was so poor that he was dismissed from school and apprenticed to a baker. He was unhappy with this career and ran away, eventually settling in Sheffield, England, where he wrote for a newspaper. The editor was threatened with prosecution and imprisonment for his political writing and fled to America. Montgomery took over the paper and was its editor for thirty-one years, during which time he was imprisoned twice for his forthright opinions. Although he was involved in various controversies during much of his life, Montgomery was a devout man and wrote hundreds of soul-stirring hymns, thirteen of which are included in *The Hymnal*.

The *Martyrdom* tune is called *Avon* in some books and has been known by some eight other titles. Its composer, Hugh Wilson, was a Scottish shoemaker and sometime schoolteacher, whose hobby was making sundials and psalm tunes. This is his only tune which has survived and is one of the most ubiquitous of English tunes, best known in America as a setting for Watts's "Alas! and Did My Savior Bleed" (No. 142).

Chapter Twelve

The Kingdom of God on Earth

Avoiding the wide and frequently disputive doctrinal implications of the phrase "The Kingdom of God," we note that in this section of *The Hymnal* are the hymns of service—the role of the believer and the church in the divine drama of God's administration of the universe. Far from the quiescent posture of waiting for God's ultimate seizure of control, the Christian is to be busily pursuing the assignments that are his to accomplish.

Here we find the urgent hymns of service, of missions, and of human relationships—in the home, the community, the nation, the world.

DISCIPLESHIP AND SERVICE

Lead On, O King Eternal (No. 437)   Ernest W. Shurtleff, 1888
Lancashire (7. 6. 7. 6. D.)   Henry Smart, 1836

Here is a hymn often classified as one of the "militant" hymns of the church, taking its place with such hymns as "Onward, Christian Soldiers" and "Stand Up for Jesus." It abounds in such words as "march," "battle," "war," "conquest"—and "peace." Its original motivation and meaning, however, are somewhat different.

The class of 1888 at Andover Theological Seminary was most fortunate in having as its class bard a genuine poet of some distinction—one who had already published three successful volumes of verse. His name is Ernest Warburton Shurtleff (1868-1917), and it was he who wrote a graduation hymn for his class that was to be used on countless other festive occasions and that has been a leading hymn of the church for more than three-quarters of a century. Mr. Shurtleff became an illustrious pastor and served churches in California, Massachusetts, and Minnesota. Later he founded a great American church in Germany and carried on an effective ministry among American students in Paris. But it is doubtful if any of his other accomplishments have approached the impact of this great hymn upon his own or future generations.

The "days of preparation" and "fields of conquest" take on new significance when one considers the purpose of the writing of this hymn. No, it is not a military hymn. On the contrary, it points out that it is "not with swords loud clashing, /Nor roll of stirring drums" that we are to gain our divine objective but "with deeds of love and mercy." It affirms the reality of sin and the necessity of the cross. Its bold theme of courageous service makes it an effective missionary challenge, particularly appealing to youth.

The tune *Lancashire*, to which the hymn is almost universally sung, was selected by Shurtleff as the most appropriate to the text. Its daring leaps and forward thrust vividly epitomize the message. Yet it was originally written by Henry Smart (1813-79) for Heber's "From Greenland's Icy Mountains." Mr. Smart, an eminent British organist and church composer, wrote it for a celebration of the 300th anniversary of the English Reformation, held in Lancashire, England, in 1835.

O Master, Let Me Walk with Thee (No. 448) Washington Gladden, 1879
Maryton (L. M.) Henry Percy Smith, 1874

One of the most prominent clergymen in America at the beginning of this century was Dr. Washington Gladden (1836-1918). He was the author of many books on a variety of subjects and occupied several important pulpits, in-

72353

cluding the First Congregational Church of Columbus, Ohio, where he had an illustrious pastorate lasting thirty-two years. It was one of his minor efforts, however, which has won for him lasting fame.

One day in 1897 Dr. Gladden decided to append a poem to an article which he was writing for his church magazine, *Sunday Afternoon*. He called it "Walking with God." Referring to it later, he said, "It had no liturgical purpose and no theological significance, but it was an honest cry of human need, of the need of divine companionship."

The eminent hymnologist, H. Augustine Smith, gives an interesting paraphrase of the hymn: "Master, may I learn to serve in comradeship with Thee; teach me how to endure hard work and responsibility. Help me to speak in clearness and love that I may win the irresponsive ones. Show me how to hold the straying and turn them back to Thee. Teach me like Thee to be patient, working in a trustful comradeship with Thee, strong in a hope that lights the unknown future, and in such peace as comes only from Thee."

During all of his life Dr. Gladden insisted that his hymn be used with no other tune than *Maryton*, by Canon Henry Percy Smith (1825-98), written for the hymn "Sun of My Soul." This wish has been granted to the extent that the tune is never heard with its original words.

This is a favorite hymn of many, including the beloved past president of the Evangelical Covenant Church, Dr. Theodore W. Anderson.

MISSIONS

O Zion, Haste, Thy Mission High   Mary Ann Thompson, 1870
Fulfilling (No. 461)
Tidings (11. 10. 11. 10. with refrain)   James Walch, 1875

Mary Ann Thompson (1834-1923) was born in London, England, but spent most of her life in Philadelphia. She was active in her church and wrote a number of hymns and poems, this being the only survivor. She tells of its writing in these words:

I wrote the greater part of the hymn, "O Zion, Haste," in the year 1868. I had written many hymns before, and one night, while I was sitting up with one of my children who was ill with typhoid fever, I thought I should like to write a missionary hymn to the tune of the hymn "Hark, Hark, My Soul! Angelic Songs Are Swelling," as I was fond of that tune, but as I could not get a refrain I liked, I left the hymn unfinished and about three years later I finished it by writing the refrain which now forms a part of it.

I do not think my hymn is ever sung to the tune for which I wrote it. Mr. Anketell (the Rev. John Anketell) told me, and I am sure he was right, that it is better for a hymn to have a tune of its own and I feel much indebted to the author of the tune *Tidings* for writing such inspiring music to my words.

Tidings, however, was written by James Walch (1837-1901) for "Hark, Hark, My Soul" and was originally called *Angelic Songs*. Later it was mated to Mrs. Thompson's text, and they have been quite inseparable. It is a strange coincidence that "O Zion, Haste," written to go with a tune associated with a text for which *Tidings* was intended, should have become so definitely linked with the latter tune.

Mrs. Thompson's closing stanza, now generally omitted, brought in the truth of the Second Coming, as follows:

He comes again, O Zion, ere thou meet Him,
  Make known to every heart His saving grace;
Let none whom He hath ransomed fail to greet Him,
  Through thy neglect, unfit to see His face.

Ye Christian Heralds, Go Proclaim   Bourne H. Draper, 1803
  (No. 467)
Missionary Chant (L. M.)   Heinrich C. Zeuner, 1832
  This unique and moving hymn consists of the last three

stanzas of a seven-stanza poem entitled "Farewell to Missionaries" written by Bourne Hall Draper (1775-1843), a young ministerial student at the Baptist Academy in Bristol, England.

Being of long meter, the hymn could be sung to many tunes. It has frequently appeared with *Duke Street* (already found five times in *The Hymnal*: Numbers 5, 162, 308, 460, and 564) but is ideally suited to *Missionary Chant*.

Charles Zeuner (1785-1857) was born in Eisleben, Saxony, the birthplace of Martin Luther. He had become a court musician in his native Saxony when he decided to come to America at the age of twenty-nine. He first became organist at famed Park Street Church in Boston, and went on to hold many fine posts in Boston and Philadelphia. He wrote hundreds of hymn tunes and other larger works and was instrumental in raising the standard of American hymns, being very critical of what he called "music of a frivolous, trifling, and may we not add profane character." He gives the following account of his writing of *Missionary Chant*: "I was sitting on one of these seats on Boston Common on a most beautiful moonlight evening, all alone, with all the world moving about me, and suddenly *Missionary Chant* was given me. I ran home as fast as ever I could and put it on paper before I should forget. That is what makes it please."

The simple eloquence of both text and tune make this a most powerful missionary commissioning hymn.

STEWARDSHIP

Savior, Thy Dying Love (No. 472)   Sylvanus D. Phelps, 1862
Something for Jesus (6. 4. 6. 4. 6. 6. 6. 4.)   Robert Lowry, 1872

Most of us speak rather glibly of the difference between

hymns and gospel songs, but we would be hard pressed to draw a definitive line between them. It is certain that since many hymns contain more gospel than the so-called gospel songs, gospel content can hardly be the criterion. Is it the style of poetry? The harmonic or melodic idiom? Or do the writers designate the song? I suppose all of these factors enter into the classification, if such a decision need be made. Some we recognize easily as having the dignity and solidity of a hymn, others as possessing the simplicity and vivacity of a gospel song. So we tend to say that hymns are never gay and gospel songs are never grave, which would be a serious dialectical error.

This hymn is a good illustration of a borderline case. Generally classified as a gospel song, it is admitted into hymnals known for their antipathy toward the gospel song. Its composer, Dr. Robert Lowry (1826-99), is known for his gospel songs (see page 90), and the harmonic structure bears out this association. Yet there is the restrained dignity of the true hymn.

Such semantic reasonings have their place in the study of hymnology, but far more important is the undeniable fact that here we have a song—simple and inauspicious—which will be used and loved for some time to come. As Dr. Lowry wrote to author Phelps on the latter's seventieth birthday: "It is worth living 70 years even if nothing comes of it but one such hymn. Happy is the man who can produce one song which the world will keep on singing after he has passed away."

Dr. Lowry published the song in his Sunday school hymnal, *Pure Gold*, which sold more than a million copies.

Dr. Sylvanus Dryden Phelps (1816-95), a New England Baptist clergyman, wrote a number of books and many song-poems, but we remember him for this one hymn. Some will also find interest in the fact that he was the father of William Lyon Phelps, famed author and English professor at Yale.

BROTHERHOOD

Rise Up, O Men of God! (No. 477)   William P. Merrill, 1911
St. Thomas (S. M.)   From "Williams' Psalmody," 1770

This stirring call to action is the work of one of America's most distinguished clergymen of recent times. Dr. William Pierson Merrill (1867-1954) was pastor for many years of the Brick Presbyterian Church of New York City, where he was able to exert a profound influence in many areas, not the least of which was that of fine church music. Of this hymn Dr. Merrill said, "Nolan R. Best, then editor of *The Continent*, happened to say to me that there was urgent need of a brotherhood hymn. . . . The suggestion lingered in my mind, and just about that time (1911) I came upon an article by Gerald Stanley Lee, entitled 'The Church of the Strong Men.' I was on one of the Lake Michigan steamers going back to Chicago for a Sunday at my own church, when suddenly this hymn came up, almost without conscious thought or effort. It has given me very deep satisfaction to have the hymn obtain such general use."

It is surely one of the better hymns of the twentieth century and one of the few American hymns to find acceptance in Great Britain and Canada.

The tune *St. Thomas*, also used in *The Hymnal* with "I Love Thy Kingdom, Lord" (No. 415), is one of the finest of the short meter tunes. It first appeared during the latter part of the eighteenth century in "Universal Psalmodist," edited by Aaron Williams (1731-76), a London schoolteacher and publisher.

MARRIAGE AND HOME

O Happy Home, Where Thou   Carl J. P. Spitta, 1833
   Art Loved (No. 485)   Trans. by Sarah B. Findlater, 1858
Alverstroke (Windsor) (11. 10. 11. 10.)   Joseph Barnby, 1883

Based on Luke 19:9, "And Jesus said unto him, This day is salvation come to this house forsomuch as he also is a son of Abraham," this hymn was first titled "Salvation is Come to This House." It is a description of life in the home of its author, Carl Johann Philipp Spitta (1801-59), the most famous German hymnist of the nineteenth century. Spitta wrote poetry from the age of eight, but felt a real call to write hymns after his conversion at the age of twenty-five. He wrote of this to a friend: "In the manner in which I formerly sang, I sing no more. To the Lord I consecrate my life and my love, and likewise my song. His love is the one great theme of all my song; to praise and exalt it worthily is the desire of the Christian singer. He gave to me song and melody; I give it back to Him."

If the hymn is true of Spitta's homelife, it is possibly more true of the life of its translator. Sarah Borthwick Findlater (1823-1907) was the translator, with her sister Jane, of 122 German hymns into English. Her daughters described her and her husband's life together as "single-eyed in their longing to serve God."

Joseph Barnby (1838-96) composed 246 hymn-tunes as well as numerous anthems and other musical works for the church. He is represented by nine hymns in *The Hymnal.* His name is synonymous with the Victorian age of church music, a style considered quite passe' in modern times, although his hymns are still popular.

THE NATION

O Beautiful for Spacious Skies (No. 492)   Katharine Lee Bates, 1904
Materna (C. M. D.)   Samuel A. Ward, 1882

In recent years there has been a concerted attack on certain public religious practices in America combined with a vigorous effort to discredit the Christian factor in our country's origins. The God-fearing nature of our founding fathers has been greatly overdrawn, they say.

"This is a myth," avers one spokesman, "that has too long influenced our society."

That there have been irreligious elements in our national life during all periods is doubtless true. Even among our early patriots there were some of the Thomas Paine variety. The proportion of their number and influence is easily recognized, however. Take, for example, those accurate thermometers of the climate of any age—our national songs.

A glance at the best-known of our patriotic songs of all periods in our national history reveals an unmistakable religious orientation even when thinking of devotion to the country.

"Battle Hymn of the Republic" is in reality a hymn of devotion to Christ. "My Country, 'Tis of Thee" has for its last stanza one of the most beautiful of patriotic prayers:

> *Our fathers' God to Thee,*
> *Author of liberty,*
> *To Thee we sing:*
> *Long may our land be bright*
> *With freedom's holy light;*
> *Protect us by Thy might,*
> *Great God, our King.*

Even our national anthem has its strong sacred strain in the little-used final stanza which exhorts us to "Praise the Power that hath made and preserved us a nation!" and reminding us of our motto, "In God is our trust."

Outstanding in this regard is the most recent of great national hymns, frequently called "America the Beautiful." Katharine Lee Bates (1859-1929) was a schoolteacher, head of the English department at Wellesley College, and this hymn was the product of a summer vacation trip. In 1893 she visited the Columbian Exposition in Chicago where the "Great White City" impressed her. It showed up in the poem in the phrase "thine alabaster cities gleam." From there she went to the Rockies, where from the summit of Pike's Peak she gazed on the magnificence of the "purple mountain majesties." A few poem ideas were entered immediately into her notebook to be completed two years later.

Former President Dwight D. Eisenhower referred to this hymn in a speech on brotherhood. And the first music projected and recovered from outer space was this hymn! Beamed at Echo I, the first communications satellite, the message was relayed back: "And crown thy good with brotherhood/From sea to shining sea."

Samuel Augustus Ward (1847-1903), composer of *Materna*, was a leading light in the musical life of Newark, New Jersey, for many years. He conducted the Orpheus Club and was a successful music dealer, but we know nothing of his work as a composer save for this hymn-tune. It was intended as a setting for the sixteenth-century hymn "O Mother Dear, Jerusalem," but was found to be a most compatible partner for Miss Bates's poem.

WORLD FRIENDSHIP AND PEACE

In Christ There Is No East or West (No. 501)   John Oxenham, 1908
St. Peter (C. M.)   Alexander R. Reinagle, 1836

In 1909 the London Missionary Society held an exposition called "The Orient in London," the chief attraction being a rather elaborate production entitled "The Pageant of Darkness and Light." The libretto, which included the text of this hymn, was written by the prominent British author and poet, John Oxenham. A mystery surrounded the writer since none of the literary set had ever met him, although his works appeared with great regularity. Even the British *Who's Who* listed no date for his birth. The fact is that "John Oxenham" was the well-concealed *nom de plume* of William Arthur Dunkerley (1852-1941), a London businessman and publisher.

Oxenham wrote some of the more distinctive hymns of the twentieth century. He is represented in *The Hymnal* by two other hymns: " 'Mid All the Traffic of the Ways" (No. 398) and "All Labor Gained New Dignity" (No. 470).

This unique hymn appears to be a rebuttal to Kipling's "East is East, and West is West, and never the twain shall meet, Till Earth and Sky stand presently at God's great Judgment Seat." It has in it the current "one world" concept and recalls the truism, "Science has made the world a neighborhood; it remains for the Church of Christ to make it a brotherhood." It is also eloquent testimony to the results of the Christian missionary movement, with the "brothers of the faith" throughout the world linked by their common knowledge of Christ.

St. Peter is one of the most ubiquitous of our hymn tunes, being used with six different texts in our hymnal and at least a dozen more in various current volumes. Its composer, Alexander Robert Reinagle (1799-1877), was part of a very musical family of Hungarian descent. His father was a noted cellist, his grandfather was known as "trumpeter to the King," and his uncle came to America and became a leading pianist-composer. He and his wife taught music in Oxford, England, where he was organist for thirty-one years at St. Peter's-in-the-East Church, doubtless the source of the tune title. This is the only surviving tune from his *Psalm Tunes for the Voice and Pianoforte*, in which it was the setting for Psalm 118, "Far better 'tis to trust in God."

Chapter Thirteen

Heaven and Homeland

*And I heard a voice from heaven, as the voice of many
waters, . . . and I heard the voice of harpers harping
with their harps: And they sung as it were a new song
before the throne . . . .*   —Revelation 14:2,3

The song of the redeemed has always been accompanied
by the upward look. The final stanza is not to be sung on
earth. It is begun on earth, to be continued in heaven, and
never to be concluded.

One of the criticisms leveled at the gospel song is that it
is too much concerned with first things and last things—
the initial salvation experience and the anticipation of
heaven. This is a just censure when such songs are not
balanced with generous use of songs of the Christian walk
and the deeper life. But for the believer, the "here and
now" is always involved with the hereafter. We are but
pilgrims and strangers in this world, moving steadily along
the road to heavenly permanency. And as we travel, we
sing songs of the homeland. This is as it should be.

√ **Behold the Host Arrayed in White** Hans Adolph Brorson, c. 1760
 √ **(No. 504)**   Trans. by Carl Doving, 1909
√ *Den store hvide flok* (8. 8. 8. 6. 12L.) Norwegian folk tune
          Arr. by Edvard Grieg (1843-1907)

One of the most-prized possessions of Scandinavian hymnody is the beloved *Den store hvide flok*. Written over two centuries ago, it has enjoyed a great increase in popularity during recent decades. It is a standard in choral literature and is widely used in solo form, yet its hymn use is uniquely confined to denominations of Scandinavian origin.

Hans Adolph Brorson (1694-1764), the author of these sublime lyrics, did not live to see their publication. They were included by his son in a collection which he called "Hans Adolph Brorson's Swan-Song" just a year after the famous Danish hymnwriter had joined "The Great White Host."

Hans Adolph was the son of a Lutheran pastor, and he, together with his two brothers, followed his father's calling. He began his hymn writing because of a lack of available hymns in his native language. In his pastorate at Tonder he had the strange experience of preaching in Danish to a congregation which knew only German hymns. The hymns he wrote to remedy that situation were among the finest the Danes have ever had.

As is common among the writers of enduring hymns, Brorson's greatest work was not done during his most successful and placid years. The sad experiences of his later life, among them the sudden passing of his beloved wife, turned his thoughts more and more heavenward. It was at this time that he penned his noble hymn-treatise on Revelation 7:13.

The association of this text with Grieg's adaptation of a Norwegian folksong is an extremely happy one, and there is little doubt that the majestic music has had much to do with the effectiveness of the hymn. Here is Edvard Grieg at his devotional best, in a style never equaled except by himself in such rare works as "I Walk with a Thousand Thoughts" and his last writings, *Psalms*, in which we find "In Heaven Above" and "God's Son Hath Set Me Free."

The fact that this masterpiece is seldom used by our

congregations is a regrettable one. Here is a song well-suited to solid unison singing, with its less-than-an-octave range and its metrical symmetry. Its length and oft-repeated phrases might suggest shortening it or using variety in its rendition.

An alternation of choral and congregational singing is very effective, particularly the antiphonal repetition of lines three and four in each five-line sequence. If this is not clear, note that we would repeat "With palms they stand" and "Who are this band" in the first eight-measure portion. One would do the same with similar phrases in each eight-measure section. The use of children's choirs is extremely effective in this type of treatment.

In Heaven All Is Gladness (No. 510)

✓ *Hos Gud är idel glädje* (7. 6. 7. 6. D.)

Johan N. Brun, 1786
Trans. composite
Oscar Ahnfelt, 1872

Johan Nordahl Brun (1745-1816) was one of a group of Norwegian evangelicals who, through song and sermon, made valiant defense of their faith against the prevailing rationalistic attacks during the early and middle nineteenth century. Born in Bynesset, he received his education at Trondhjem and Copenhagen. He was a powerful preacher and a gifted poet—one of conservative Christianity's strongest voices. Dominating all his efforts was a deep love for the Bible, acquired during childhood, when he read the Scriptures through twice before the age of eleven.

Oscar Ahnfelt (1813-82), composer of the tune, was known as the "spiritual troubador," who, in the words of Lina Sandell, "sang the songs into the hearts of the people." He wrote words for many hymns but was best known for the melodies which he composed and sang to the accompaniment of a unique ten-string guitar—his own invention.

Ahnfelt was born near Eslöv, Sweden. He received his elementary education from his older brothers, then went to the university at Lund. His prevailing interest in music took him to Stockholm, where he studied voice and theory, later becoming an instructor. While in Stockholm, he came under the influence of the great religious revival and felt a real spiritual void in his life. That void was gloriously filled on Easter Sunday morning in 1841 when, after a ringing sermon by Rosenius on "The Power of the Resurrection," Ahnfelt found peace of soul.

He joined the revival movement, with Rosenius as his close friend and spiritual adviser. Soon he was traveling on a full-time basis—singing, playing and preaching. It was during this time that he met and married Clara Strömberg, the daughter of a military man. She became a great help to him, writing many songs of her own and exerting a wide spiritual influence.

Financial rewards for an itinerant singer are not great, and the Ahnfelts were frequently pressed to meet their most meager of needs. When it came to publishing the many songs he wrote, it was simply impossible. At this point there came help from a most remarkable source. None other than Jenny Lind, "the Swedish nightingale," became enamored with Ahnfelt's music and in 1850 supplied the funds for their publication. The title page read "Spiritual Songs to be sung to the accompaniment of piano or guitar, composed by Oscar Ahnfelt and reverently dedicated by him to the great songstress, Jenny Lind."

Rosenius and Ahnfelt found many influential people opposed to their evangelistic efforts. At one time they even petitioned King Karl XV to put an end to Ahnfelt's singing and preaching. The king would not do so until he had heard him, and so the "spiritual troubador" played a command performance at the royal palace. He sang a new hymn, with words by Lina Sandell, and the monarch, visibly moved, reached out his hand and exclaimed, "You may sing as much as you desire in both my kingdoms!"

Chapter Fourteen

Children's Hymns

*Out of the mouth of babes . . . thou hast perfected
praise.*   —Matthew 21:16

Childhood is always a time of spontaneous singing. It is
also a time for teaching, both in and through singing. The
art of true praise can be acquired best through early training. Simple and tasteful songs taught during the early form-
ative years build an appreciation for worthy church music.
Secular-styled ditties and jingles with sacred implications
can do little but confuse and cheapen. The teaching of
salient truths through songs is one of Christian education's most potent tools. God taught Moses this technique
when He said, "Write this song, and teach it to the people
of Israel; put it in their mouths, that this song may be a
witness for me. . . . This song shall confront them as a witness (for it will live unforgotten in the mouths of their
descendants)" (Deuteronomy 31:19 and 21, RSV).

In making use of the fine selections in *The Hymnal* for
children, we must remember that these are songs which
are planned for certain age levels. They are songs which the
children will *grow out of*. The use of standard hymns should
not be neglected, for these are hymns which the child will
grow into.

I Think When I Read That Sweet Story   Jemima T. Luke, 1841
(No. 537)
Sweet Story (Irregular)   Greek folksong
                                    Arr. by William B. Bradbury, 1859

A question often asked by those interested in the study of hymnology is: "Which came first, the tune or the text?" It's not a particularly important question, for we are not greatly concerned over who wooed whom, provided they are well wed. However, it would seem that the majority of composers find their inspiration in a text, although hymnal compilers may find occasion to exchange them a bit.

There are a number of cases where the reverse procedure was followed and a melody suggested the poem. Many of Fanny Crosby's hymns were thus written, e. g., "Blessed Assurance" (No. 322) and "Close to Thee" (No. 391). And such is the case with this children's song.

Miss Jemima Thompson (1813-1906), who later became Mrs. Samuel Luke, was a teacher. One day while visiting the Normal Infant School at Gray's Inn Road, London, she heard an old Greek tune which haunted her for days. She thought it should have appropriate words and perused the works of Watts and other hymnwriters for a suitable text in the right meter. Finding none, she wrote one herself! It was during an hour's ride on a stagecoach that the inspiration came, and it was written in pencil on the back of an old envelope.

Later she taught the hymn to her Sunday school pupils, who loved it immediately. Miss Thompson's father was superintendent of the Sunday school and was very interested in hymns. One day he offered a prize of twenty pounds for a new hymn. The children sang their newly learned song for him.

"Where did you find that hymn?" he asked.

"Jemima wrote it!" the children chorused.

The original hymn had just the three stanzas which are included in *The Hymnal*, but she wrote two more at a later time to give the hymn a missionary tone. Missions was her all-absorbing interest, and although her attempt to become a missionary herself was frustrated by illness, she continued to serve the cause in many ways. She was editor of the first missionary publication for children, called *The Missionary Repository*, and was a friend of Miss Mary Moffatt, the daughter of pioneer missionary James Moffatt and later the wife of David Livingstone.

The concluding stanzas are:

But thousands and thousands who wander and fall,
Never heard of that heavenly home;
I wish they could know there is room for them all,
And that Jesus has bid them to come.

I long for the joy of that glorious time,
The sweetest and brightest and best,
When the dear little children of every clime
Shall crowd to His arms and be blest.

Chapter Fifteen

Special Seasons and Services

*... therefore we will sing ... songs ... all the days of
our life in the house of the Lord.*   —Isaiah 38:20

For those churches which follow the full liturgical calendar there are appropriate songs for every Sunday of the year, quite easily selected by consulting the recommended texts for that day. But even for these there are special days and occasions not included in the Church Year. These are grouped together in *The Hymnal* for our convenience. Some of the finest hymns were written for these particular occasions.

THANKSGIVING AND HARVEST

Come, Ye Thankful People, Come (No. 541)   Henry Alford, 1844
St. George's Windsor (7. 7. 7. 7. D.)   George J. Elvey, 1858

Henry Alford (1810-71) was one of the busiest men of his time. For many years he was the beloved dean of Canterbury Cathedral. He wrote fifty books, including his famed four-volume *Greek Testament* and such diverse efforts as a translation of Homer's *Odyssey* and a collection of *English Descriptive Poetry*. Haeussler characterizes him as "theologian, scholar, poet, writer, artist, and musician ... one of the most gifted men of his day." No churchman was more in demand than he.

Yet, in spite of all his horizontal contacts with the world about him, Dean Alford allowed nothing to keep him from the all-important vertical relationship with his Lord.

It is said that at the end of each day's work, as well as after every meal, he would stand, and, looking heavenward, thank God for the blessings he had received. This spirit of perpetual praise is well voiced in this famed harvest hymn.

Alford was a brilliant student from his very earliest days, but his consecration more than matched his erudition. On his sixteenth birthday he wrote in his Bible, "I do this day, in the presence of God and my soul, renew my covenant with God, and solemnly determine henceforth to become His and to do His work as far as in me lies."

He cherished one desire which was never realized: that of visiting the Holy Land. But when he died, the following words, in Latin, were inscribed on his tombstone: *Deversorium viatoris proficientis Hierosolymam*—"The inn of a pilgrim traveling to Jerusalem."

His other classic hymn, "Ten Thousand Times Ten Thousand" (No. 179), which E. E. Ryden calls "A Vision of the Final Triumph," was sung at the dean's funeral by a multitude assembled in the Canterbury churchyard.

The tune associated with this hymn, *St. George's Windsor*, matches the superlative quality of the text. Its composer, George Job Elvey (1816-93), was also associated with Canterbury Cathedral, having begun his career as a choirboy there. At the age of nineteen he was appointed as organist of St. George's Chapel, Windsor, a post which he held for forty-seven years until his retirement. This was the church of the royal family and the site, according to tradition, of King Arthur's famed Round Table. Many honors came to Elvey, including knighthood.

Of him a contemporary said, "No one could be long in his presence without being struck by his devout, religious spirit, and it was this spirit that went into all of his work."

Two other strong tunes by Sir George are to be found in *The Hymnal: Diademata*, used with the majestic hymn "Crown Him with Many Crowns" (No. 168), and *St. Crispin*, associated with Tennyson's "Strong Son of God" (No. 136) and "O Grant Us Light" (No. 560). The latter tune, incidentally, was written for "Just As I Am" (No. 250), and is felt by many to surpass the Bradbury tune.

Thanks to God for My Redeemer   August Ludvig Storm, 1891
    (No. 543)   Trans. by Carl E. Backstrom (1901-   )
Tack, O Gud (8. 7. 8. 7. D.)   J. A. Hultman (1861-1942)

One of the favorite songs of Swedish heritage is this cheerful enumeration of the various areas of thanksgiving. Notable is the inclusion of negative items as the objects of praise, such as "dark and dreary fall," "what Thou dost deny," "storms," "pain," and "thorns." All of these were experienced in good measure by the author, August Ludvig Storm (1862-1914), who was stricken at the age of thirty-seven with a severe back ailment which left him partially paralyzed. Storm was born in the village of Motala, moving to Stockholm when but a year old. He attended business and agricultural colleges and worked for several years in the business world. In his mid-twenties he tired of the gay life he was leading and was converted through the ministry of the Salvation Army. He later joined the Army and served as lieutenant in charge of finance for the remainder of his life.

Of considerably greater interest is the life of the composer of this and many other popular Swedish-American tunes, John Alfred Hultman (1861-1942). Popularly known as "The Sunshine Singer," Hultman was a successful pastor, poet, composer, teacher, organist, pianist, manufacturer of pianos, and publisher of sacred music. He was born in Sweden and emigrated with his family to America when he was but eight years of age. He began his preaching and singing career while yet in his teens and for more than sixty years divided his time between Sweden and America in concertizing in his unique way. These programs were characterized by great variety and contrast, many interspersed remarks and anecdotes, frequent trips from piano to organ and back again as he played solos or accompanied himself, and dramatic pauses to polish his pince-nez glasses. These were far from the traditional formal recitals, and he broke many of the rules for formal decorum, but here was—as his biographer, Nils Lund, put it—"A gospel troubador, and 'the common people heard him gladly.' "

"Oh, that I could like the skylark warble, and sing bright sunshine into the world," ran one of his favorite songs. Indeed, the words "sunshine" and "joy" occur so frequently in the more than five hundred songs he wrote and sang that one would suppose that this was how he earned his title as "The Sunshine Singer." "Not so," said Pastor Hultman to a reporter for a Stockholm journal. "They gave me that name during the days of the great strike in 1909. I sang then in Stockholm to overflow audiences in many places. Great crowds could not find seats but stood outside in the sunshine and listened. So they called me 'The Sunshine Singer,' " adding with a twinkle, "and one can get a worse name than 'The Sunshine Singer.' "

J. A. Hultman continued singing to the very end. His "farewell" and "final" concert tours were legendary, but it was at one of these farewells that he left this earthly scene. It was in the Covenant church of Burbank, California. He had just begun the concert and was seated at the piano, giving voice to one of his favorites, Philip Phillips' "The Grand Old Story." The first stanza is an invitation to "Come and hear the grand old story,/Story of the ages past,/All earth's annals far surpassing;/Story that ever shall last." At the word "story" his voice faltered. While he played the music, he kept repeating over and over "story . . . story." His son, Paul—who, incidentally, later became a famed concert artist—rushed to the platform to catch his father as he collapsed. He never finished that song in this life. J. A. Hultman had realized his oft-sung wish:

> *Oh, that I could like the skylark warble,*
> *And sing bright sunshine into the world,*
> *Then disappear in the glowing sunset,*
> *And fall asleep in Thy bosom, Lord.*

THE NEW YEAR

Another Year Is Dawning (No. 547) Frances Ridley Havergal, 1874
Aurelia (7. 6. 7. 6. D.)   Samuel S. Wesley, 1864

In January of 1874 the many friends of Frances Ridley Havergal (1836-79) received a New Year's greeting with the heading "A Happy New Year! Ever Such May It Be!" Following this appeared the full text of this, her latest hymn-poem. Surely this was a greeting card not to be read and then tossed aside! For these many years it has remained the finest New Year's prayer of consecration of all.

Miss Havergal could well be called the hymnist of consecration. The rich outpourings of her prolific pen seem to be anointed with the perfume of purity, of dedication of heart and life. There is a reason. Hers are hymns which were lived before they were written. Her life was one of constant and complete commitment, and her poems seem to articulate each attitude and act of dedication.

Her best-known hymn, "Take My Life and Let It Be" (No. 281), is most minutely autobiographical in its every quatrain. Life, time, voice, lips, silver and gold, intellect, and love—all were hers in most generous portion. She was an accomplished classical pianist and vocalist. Her speaking and intellectual talents were prodigious, including proficiency in seven languages and the memorization of the entire New Testament, Psalms, Isaiah, and the Minor Prophets! She was the possessor of wealth, culture, and good breeding. But all were hers to give. And she gave!

Her basic hymnic talent was doubtless an inherited one. Her father, the Rev. W. H. Havergal, was one of the pioneers of modern hymnody, particularly on the musical side of the page. With his help, Frances was reading and playing from the hymnal at the age of three and was able to read and write a year later. He called her "Little Quicksilver," but she was anything but mercurial in her disposition, which, they say, was always sunny, despite a lifetime of ill health. Her natural radiance took on a deeper hue at the age of fourteen when she had a powerful religious experience. Of this she wrote, "I committed my soul to the Savior, and earth and heaven seemed brighter from that moment." Through that commitment Frances Ridley Havergal was enabled to brighten countless other lives.

On the tune side of this hymn we have a familiar name—"Wesley." But this is not Charles or John, neither of whom are represented by music composition. This is Samuel Sebastian Wesley (1810-76), grandson of Charles, named for his father Samuel and his father's favorite composer, Johann Sebastian Bach. Various biographers have dubbed him "the Anglican composer *par excellence*," "the greatest writer of church music in the nineteenth century," and "the best English organist of his time."

His career as organist began at the age of sixteen and continued for the next fifty years in some of the finest churches and cathedrals in Britain. His sacred choral compositions are among the best England has produced and deserve a much wider use than they now enjoy. He was a lifelong crusader for worthy church music. *Aurelia*, written for the wedding hymn "The Voice That Breathed O'er Eden," has been most closely associated with "The Church's One Foundation" (No. 418).

Index

Index

This is a composite index including hymn titles; tune names; authors, composers, and translators; and other items. Hymn titles are given within quotation marks, and tune names are italicized. The names of authors, composers, and translators and other items of a general nature are set in Roman type.

A

"A Mighty Fortress Is Our God," 76

Abney, Sir Thomas and Lady, 87

"According to Thy Gracious Word," 97

Adams, John Quincy, 6

"Again Thy Glorious Sun Doth Rise," 42

Ahnfelt, Oscar, 79, 111

"Alas! and Did My Savior Bleed," 87, 97

Alexander, Charles, 2

Alexander, James W., 48

Alford, 30, 77

Alford, Henry, 117

"All Glory, Laud, and Honor," 46

"All Hail the Power of Jesus' Name," 51

"All Hail to Thee, O Blessed Morn!" 17, 41

"All Labor Gained New Dignity," 108

"All People That on Earth Do Dwell," 16

"Almighty God, Thy Word Is Cast," 61

Alverstroke (Windsor), 105

"Am I a Soldier of the Cross?" 87

"Amazing Grace! How Sweet the Sound," 69

Ambrose, 2

Amen, 13

"America the Beautiful," 11

"Ancient of Days, Who Sittest Throned in Glory," 13

Anderson, Dr. Theodore W., 100

Andover Theological Seminary, 98

Anketell, Rev. John, 101

"Another Year Is Dawning," 121

Ar Hyd Y Nos, 7

Arian Heresy, 2

"Art Thou Weary, Art Thou Languid?" 50

"As Pants the Hart for Cooling Streams," 32

"As with Gladness Men of Old," 43
Assurance, 78
Atlantic Monthly, 54
Aurelia, 121
Austrian Hymn, 62
Avon, 97
"Awake, My Soul, Stretch Every Nerve," 96

B

Babcock, Maltbie D., 32
Bach, Johann Sebastian, 3, 17, 32, 46, 48, 94, 122
Backstrom, Carl E., 119
Baltimore, Maryland, 33
Barnby, Joseph, 105
Barnum, P. T., 59
Barrows, Cliff, 20
Bates, Katharine Lee, 105
Bathurst, William H., 75
Battle Hymn of the Republic, 53
Bay Psalm Book, 1
Beautiful River, 7
Beecher, 7
Beecher, Henry Ward, 2, 71
Beethoven, Ludwig van, 3, 22, 62, 95
"Behold the Host Arrayed in White," 109
Belcher, Joseph, 94
Belmont, 61
Benson, 71
Bernard of Clairvaux, 48
Best, Nolan R., 104
Bithynia, 21
"Blest Be the Tie That Binds," 94
"Blessed Assurance, Jesus Is Mine!" 78, 115

Bliss, P. P., 82
Blott en dag, 79
Boberg, Carl, 18
Bonar, Horatius, 66
Boston, 102
Bourgeois, Louis, 16
Bradbury, William B., 37, 67, 74, 115
"Bread of the World in Mercy Broken," 29
"Break Thou the Bread of Life," 24
"Breathe on Me, Breath of God," 57
Breed, 71
Brick Presbyterian Church, 33, 104
Brighton, England, 43, 68
Bristol, England, 44, 102
Brooklyn, New York, 90
Brorson, Hans Adolph, 109
Brun, Johan N., 111
Bryant, 3
Bunyan, 3
Burns, 36

C

California, 99
Calvin, John, 34
Cambridge, 21
"Can We Forbear to Sing," 55
Canonbury, 59
Canterbury Cathedral, 117
Cardiff, Wales, 82
Carter Lane Church, 55
Cawood, John, 61
Charlemagne, 46
Chautauqua, 7

Chautauqua, Lake, 23
Chicago, Illinois, 5, 82, 85, 104
Chopin, 59
"Christ Is Made the Sure Foundation," 92
Christian Endeavor Society, 26
Christiansen, Dr. F. M., 80
Church of England, 93
Churchill, Sir Winston, 53
Cincinnati, Ohio, 91
Civil War, 54
Clark, Mrs. Frances E., 26
Clark, James F., 54
Clement of Alexandria, 6
"Close to Thee," 115
Codner, Elizabeth, 74
Columbus, Ohio, 100
"Come Thou Fount of Every Blessing," 25
"Come to Calvary's Holy Mountain," 47
"Come unto Me, Ye Weary," 44
"Come, We That Love the Lord," 86
"Come, Ye Faithful, Raise the Strain," 51
"Come, Ye Thankful People, Come," 45, 117
Common Meter, 7
Copyrights, 14
Coronation, 51
Council of Toledo, Spain, 64
Covenant Press, 5
Cowper, William, 35, 70
Croft, William, 31
Crosby, Fanny (Mrs. Alexander Van Alstyne), 6, 78, 115

"Crown Him with Many Crowns," 45, 119
Crüger, Johann, 17

D

Dahle, John, 48
Darwall, 7
"David's Psalmer," 56
"Day by Day Thy Mercies, Lord, Attend Me," 79
"Day Is Dying in the West," 23, 29
Denison University, 63
Dennis, 94
Den store hvide flok, 109
Diadem, 53
Diademata, 45, 119
Dix, 7, 43
Dix, William C., 43
Doane, William H., 63
Doddridge, Philip, 96
Donne, John, 36
Doving, Carl, 109
Doxology, 8, 17
Draper, Bourne H., 102
Duffield, 71
Duke Street, 8, 102
Dundee, 35
Dunkerley, William Arthur, 108
Dykes, John Bacchus, 6, 28, 66, 77

E

Ebenezer, 10
Echo I, 107
Egypt, 77
Ehrenborg, Betty, 17
Eilenburg, Saxony, 18
Ein' Feste Burg, 7
Eisenhower, Dwight D., 107

Eisleben, Saxony, 102
Ekman, 20
Ellers, 26
Ellerton, John, 26
Elliot, Emily E. Steele, 43
Elliott, Charlotte, 67
Ellor, James, 53
Elvey, George J., 44, 117
"Encamped Along the Hills of Light," 11
Ephraim, 2
Evan, 75
Evangel, 63
Evangelical Covenant Church of America, Preface, 5, 100
Even Me, 74
Evening Praise (Chautauqua), 23

F

"Faith Is the Victory," 11
"Father, Again in Jesus' Name We Meet," 27
Fawcett, John, 94
Federal Street, 7
Findlater, Sarah B., 105
"'Follow Me!' A Call So Tender," 64
Frankfort, 16
Frankfort, 17, 41
Franzén, 17
"From Greenland's Icy Mountains," 29, 51, 99
Frykman, Nils, 83
"Fugue in E-flat Major," 32

G

Gardiner, William, 61
Geneva, 16

Genevan Psalter, 16, 34
George II, 36
Gerhardt, Paul, 48
Gilmore, Joseph H., 37
Gladden, Washington, 99
Glasgow, Scotland, 44
"Glorious Things of Thee Are Spoken," 70
"God Moves in a Mysterious Way," 35
"God of the Nations," 35
"God of the Prophets," 35
"God, That Madest Earth and Heaven," 29
"God's Son Hath Set Me Free," 110
Gottschalk, Louis M., 58
Graham, Billy, 20
"Great God, We Sing That Mighty Hand," 96
Greensleeves, 16, 44
Gregory the Great, 92
Grieg, Edvard, 109

H

Haeussler, Armin, 36, 117
Hamburg, 8
Handel, 3
Hankey, Katherine, 63
"Hark, Hark, My Soul," 51, 101
Harrisburg, Pennsylvania, 26
Hartford, Connecticut, 60
Hassler, Hans Leo, 48
Hatch, Edwin, 57
Havergal, Frances Ridley, 58, 77, 121
Havergal, William H., 58, 75, 122
Hawks, Annie S., 90

Haydn, 3, 59, 62
He Leadeth Me, 37
"He Leadeth Me! O Blessed Thought!" 37
Heber, Reginald, 28, 99
Hedborn, Samuel J., 17
Heidelberg, 58
"Hide Not Thy Face, O My Savior," 80
Hine, Stuart K., 19
Holden, Oliver, 51
Holmes, Oliver Wendell, 3
"Holy Ghost, with Light Divine," 58
"Holy, Holy, Holy! Lord God Almighty," 28
"Holy Majesty! Before Thee," 17
"Holy Spirit, Faithful Guide," 59
Hopkins, Edward J., 26
Hos Gud är idel glädje, 111
"How Firm a Foundation," 12
"How Precious Is the Book Divine," 95
"How Sweet the Name of Jesus Sounds," 70
"How Wonderful It Is," 85
Howe, Julia Ward, 53
Hultman, J. A., 119
Hymn to joy, 22, 59

I

"I Greet Thee, Who My Sure Redeemer Art," 34
"I Have a Friend Who Loveth Me," 85
"I Have a Future All Sublime," 85

"I Heard the Voice of Jesus Say," 9, 66
"I Love Thy Kingdom, Lord," 104
"I Need Thee Every Hour," 90
"I Sing with Joy and Gladness," 83, 85
"I Think When I Read That Sweet Story," 115
"Immortal Love, Forever Full," 96
"In Christ There Is No East or West," 9, 107
"In Heaven Above," 110
"In Heaven All Is Gladness," 111
Indexes, 5-11
It is well with my soul, 82

J

Jamestown, New York, 23
"Jerusalem, Lift Up Thy Voice!" 42
"Jesus, Lord and Precious Savior," 42
"Jesus, Lover of My Soul," 71
"Jesus Shall Reign," 8, 87
"Jesus, Where'er Thy People Meet," 36
"John Brown's Body," 54
John of Damascus, 50
Johnson, E. Gustav, 6, 19, 83
Johnson, Gustaf F., Preface
Johnson, Obed, Preface, 80
"Joy to the World!" 87
"Joyful, Joyful, We Adore Thee," 22
Julian, 88
"Just As I Am, Without One Plea," 67 119

K

"K" in Rippon's "Selection," 12
Ken, Thomas, 16
Kelly, Thomas, 51
Kethe, William, 16
King Karl XV, 112
Kipling, Rudyard, 108
Knapp, Joseph Fairchild, 79
Knapp, Mrs. Joseph F., 78
Kocher, Conrad, 43

L

Lake Ontario, 33
Lancashire, 50
Lathbury, Mary A., 23
"Lead On, O King Eternal," 51, 98
Leicester, England, 62
"Lift Up Your Heads, Ye Mighty Gates," 39
Lind, Jenny, 112
Lindeman, Ludvig M., 47
"List to the Gospel Resounding," 85
Livingstone, David, 116
Ljuva röst, 64
Lockport, New York, 33
London, 22, 101
London Missionary Society, 107
Long Meter, 7
Longfellow, Henry Wadsworth, 3, 16, 41
"Look, Ye Saints, the Sight Is Glorious," 51
"Lord, Dismiss Us with Thy Blessing," 95
"Lord, I Hear of Showers of Blessing," 74

"Lord, Thou Hast Been Our Refuge," 32
"Lost in the Night," 80
Louis I, 46
Loven Herren, 7
Lövgren, Oscar, Preface, 80 83
Lowell, James Russell, 3
Lowry, Robert, 86, 90, 102
Luke, Jemima T., 115
Lund, Nils, 120
Luther, Martin, 1, 48, 102

M

Magnificat, 20
Malan, Dr. Caesar, 68
Malpas, Middlewich, and Natwich Choral Association, 26
Marching to Zion, 86
Margaret, 42
Marsh, Simeon B., 71
Martyn, 71
Martyrdom, 97
Maryton, 99
Mason, Lowell, 6, 21, 69, 94
Massachusetts, 99
Materna, 105
Mathams, Walter J., 77
Matheson, George, 88
Matthews, Timothy R., 42
Mendebras, 21
Mendelssohn, 3, 17, 18
Mercy, 58
Merrill, William P., 104
Metropolitan Life Insurance Company, 79
" 'Mid All the Traffic of the Ways," 108
Miles Lane, 53

"Mine Eyes Have Seen the Glory," 53

Minneapolis, Minnesota, 65

Minnesota, 65, 85, 99

Missionary Chant, 102

Moffatt, James, 116

Montgomery, James, 47, 97

Moody Bible Institute, 63

Moody, Dwight L., 2 63, 66, 68, 82

Mozart, 3, 62

"My Country, 'Tis of Thee," 106

"My Soul Now Magnifies the Lord," 20

N

Naar mit øie, traet af møie, 47

Nachtstuck, 59

Naegeli, Hans G., 94

Naples, Italy, 33

Neale, John M., 46, 50, 92

Need, 90

Nettleton, 25

Nettleton, Asahel, 26

New York City, 33, 60, 69, 104

Newton, John, 36, 69, 77

Nicaea, 28

Nicolai, Philip, 17, 41

Ninth Symphony (Beethoven), 23, 59

North Park College, 19

Nova Vita, 58

"Now Let Every Tongue Adore Thee," 17

"Now Thank We All Our God," 17

Nu är jag nöjd, 83

Nun danket, 17

O

"O Beautiful for Spacious Skies," 11, 105

"O Bride of Christ, Rejoice," 42

"O Day of Rest and Gladness," 21

"O for a Closer Walk with God," 36

"O for a Faith That Will Not Shrink," 75

"O God, Our Help in Ages Past," 31, 87

"O Grant Us Light," 119

"O Happy Day, That Fixed My Choice," 96

"O Happy Home, Where Thou Art Loved," 105

"O Love That Wilt Not Let Me Go," 88

"O Master, Let Me Walk with Thee," 99

"O Mighty God, When I Behold the Wonder," 18

"O Morning Star! How Fair and Bright," 17

"O Mother Dear, Jerusalem," 107

"O Sacred Head, Now Wounded," 48

O store Gud, 18

"O Thou, in Whose Presence My Soul Takes Delight," 55

"O Zion, Haste, Thy Mission High Fulfilling," 100

Old Hundredth, 8, 16

Olney Hymns, 36, 70

Olson, Ernst W., 41

"Onward, Christian Soldiers," 98

"Open the Gates of the Temple," 79

"Our Helper, God, We Bless Thy Name," 96

"Our Mighty God Works Mighty Wonders," 84

Oxenham, John, 9, 107

Oxford, England, 58 108

P

Page format, 11

Palestine, 74, 77

Palmberg, 20

Paraguay, 77

Park Street Church, 102

Parker, Dr. Edwin Pond, 60

Passion Chorale, 48

Peace, Albert L., 88

"Peace, Perfect Peace," 90

Perronet, Edward, 51

Phelps, Sylvanus D., 103

Phelps, William Lyon, 104

Philadelphia, Pennsylvania, 37, 101, 102

Phillips, Philip, 79, 120

Pike's Peak, 107

Pilgrims, 51

Pliny the Younger, 21

Pontus, 21

"Praise God from Whom All Blessings Flow," 8, 17

Prokhanoff, I. S., 19

Psalter, 1

Q

Queen Elizabeth II, 16

Queen (Bloody) Mary, 16

Queen Victoria, 89

R

Rathbun, 7

Reed, Andrew, 58

Reeves, Jeremiah B., 28

Regent Square, 51, 92

Reinagle, Alexander R., 107

Richmond, Virginia, 54

"Ring Out, Wild Bells," 45

Rinkart, Martin, 17, 18

Rippon, John, 51, 55

"Rise Up, O Men of God!" 104

Robinson, Robert, 25

Rochester, New York, 38

Rodeheaver, Homer, 2

Rosenius, Carl Olof, 112

Ryden, Ernest Edwin, 3, 79, 118

S

"Safely Through Another Week," 70

St. Agnes, 30

St. Anne, 31

"St. Anne's Fugue," 32

St. Clement's Church, 32

St. Crispin, 45, 119

St. George's Windsor, 45, 117

St. Margaret, 88

St. Mary Woolnoth, 70

St. Paul, Minnesota, 65

St. Peter, 9, 107

St. Theodulph, 7, 46

St. Thomas, 104

Salvation Army, 119

Sandell, Lina, 79, 111

Sånger och Psalmer, 13

Sankey, Ira D., 2, 63, 66, 82

Sanningsvittnet, 20

"Savior, Again to Thy Dear Name We Raise," 26

"Savior, Thy Dying Love," 102

Schiller, 23
Schumann, 3
Scott, Rev. E. P., 52
Scottish Psalter, 35
"See Israel's Gentle Shepherd Stand," 96
"See the Conqueror Mounts in Triumph," 51
"Send Forth, O God, Thy Light and Truth," 6
Serenity, 96
Shakespeare, William, 16
Shea, George Beverly, 19
"Shepherd of Tender Youth," 6
Sheppard, Franklin L., 32
Sherburne, New York, 72
Sherwin, William F., 23
Short Meter, 7
Shrubsole, William, 53
Shurtleff, Ernest W., 98
Sibelius, Jean, 3
Skogsbergh, Erik A., 2, 66
Skoog, A. L., 3, 65
Smart, Sir George Thomas, 93
Smart, Henry, 50, 92, 93, 98
Smith, H. Augustine, 100
Smith, Henry Percy, 99
Something for Jesus, 103
Spafford, Horatio G., 82
Spiess, Johann Martin, 57
"Spirit Divine, Attend Our Prayer," 59
Spitta, Carl J. P., 105
"Stand Fast for Christ Thy Savior," 77
"Stand Up for Jesus," 98
Stebbins, George C., 24
Steffe, John William, 53
Stephen of Mar Saba, 50

Stockholm, Sweden, 112, 119
Stony Brook Bible Conference, 20
Storm, August Ludvig, 119
Strassburg, 34
"Strong Son of God, Immortal Love," 45, 119
Stuttgart, Germany, 44
"Sun of My Soul," 100
Sunday, Billy, 2
"Sunset and Evening Star," 45
Sutherland, 71
Swabia, 57
Swain, Joseph, 55
Swedish, 5, 6, 56
Sweet Story, 115
Symphony No. 93 (Haydn), 59
Syracuse, New York, 33

T

Tack, O Gud, 119
"Take My Life and Let It Be," 121
Te Deum, 24
Telford, 71
"Tell Me the Old, Old Story," 63
"Ten Thousand Times Ten Thousand," 78, 118
Tennyson, Alfred Lord, 3, 28, 45, 119
Terra Beata, 32
Tersanctus, 22, 24, 29
Teschner, Melchior, 46
"Thanks to God for My Redeemer," 119
"The Church in the Wildwood," 4

"The Church's One Foundation," 122
The Courtship of Miles Standish, 16
"The Day of Resurrection," 50
"The Day Thou Gavest, Lord, Is Ended," 27
The First Nowell, 7
"The Highest Joy That Can Be Known," 85
The Holy Year, 22
The Last Hope, 60
"The Lord Be with Us," 27
The Merry Wives of Windsor, 16
"The Son of God Goes Forth to War," 29
"The Spirit Breathes Upon the Word," 10, 36
"The Voice That Breathed O'er Eden," 122
Theodulph of Orleans, 46
"There Is a Fountain," 36
Thirty Years' War, 18
"This Is My Father's World," 32
Thompson, Mary Ann, 101
"Thou Didst Leave Thy Throne," 42
Tidings, 101
Ton-Y-Botel, 7, 10
Torrey, R. J., 2
Toulon, 34
Trajan, 21
Trentham, 58
Trinity College, 21
Truro, 39

U

Unwin, Morley, 36

V

Van Alstyne, Mrs. Alexander (Fanny Crosby), 78
Van Dyke, Henry, 22, 33
Var hälsad, sköna morgonstund, 41
Våra Psalm- och Sångdiktare, Preface, 80
Värmland, Sweden, 65, 83
Vienna, 23
Ville duHavre, 82
Vincent, John H., 23
Virginia Harmony, 71
Vox Dilecti, 9, 66

W

Wachet Auf, 17
Walch, James, 101
Waldenström, P. P., 20
Wallace, William V., 96
Wallin, Johan Olof, 17, 41
Ward, Samuel A., 106
Warmingham, Osbert W., 31
Washington, D. C., 54
"Watch, My Soul, and Pray," 42
Watchman and Reflector, 38
Watts, Isaac, 29, 31, 86
Weber, 3
Weissel, Georg, 39
Wellesley College, 107
Wells, Marcus, 59
Wennerberg, 55
Wennerberg, Gunnar, 55
Wesley, Charles, 2, 6, 71, 122
Wesley, John, Preface, 2, 26, 51, 88, 122
Wesley, Samuel S., 121
Westminster Abbey, 22
"What a Friend We Have in Jesus," 9

"What Child Is This?" 44
"When I Survey the Wondrous Cross," 8, 87
"When My Lord Is Dear to Me," 85
"When Peace, Like a River, Attendeth My Way," 82
Whitefield, George, 26
Whittier, John Greenleaf, 3, 96
Williams, Aaron, 104
Williams College, 22
"Williams' Psalmody," 104
Williams, Ralph Vaughan, 16, 32
Williams, Thomas, 39

Wilson, Hugh, 97
Windsor, 105
Winkworth, Catherine, 18, 39
Woodworth, 67
Wordsworth, Christopher, 3, 21, 51
Wordsworth, William, 21, 36
World War II, 38
Wyeth, John, 25

Y

Yale University, 59, 104
"Ye Christian Heralds, Go Proclaim," 102

Z

Zeuner, Heinrich C., 102